About This Report

To improve its understanding of the Department of Defense's (DoD's) officer professional military education (PME) system, Congress asked DoD to develop a broad overview of the officer PME system in Section 576 of the 2021 National Defense Authorization Act. The Office of the Under Secretary of Defense for Personnel and Readiness in turn asked RAND National Defense Research Institute researchers to aid in fulfilling this request. In response, the researchers developed this report, which describes the DoD officer education system, reviews how it operates, compares it with civilian institutions, analyzes effects of possible changes, and identifies opportunities to further align the system to DoD's needs. The report also contains detailed factual information about each educational institution in the system. The report should be of interest to policymakers in Congress and DoD as they develop and modify policies that govern this system.

The research reported here was completed in February 2023 and underwent security review with the sponsor and the Defense Office of Prepublication and Security Review before public release.

RAND National Security Research Division

This research was sponsored by the Under Secretary of Defense for Personnel and Readiness and conducted within the Personnel, Readiness, and Health Program of the RAND National Security Research Division (NSRD), which operates the National Defense Research Institute (NDRI), a federally funded research and development center sponsored by the Office of the Secretary of Defense, the Joint Staff, the Unified Combatant Commands, the Navy, the Marine Corps, the defense agencies, and the defense intelligence enterprise.

For more information on the RAND Personnel, Readiness, and Health Program, see www.rand.org/nsrd/prh or contact the director (contact information is provided on the webpage).

Acknowledgments

We are grateful for the support of Gary Schaub and Eric Russi of the Office of the Under Secretary of Defense for Personnel and Readiness, Force Education and Training, who provided guidance and assistance throughout the study. We thank Daniel Ginsberg, Molly McIntosh, Lisa Harrington, and Harry Thie for their thoughtful reviews of drafts of this report. We appreciate the military services, military educational institutions, and the selected civilian institutions for providing information throughout the course of this research.

Intellectual Firepower

A REVIEW OF PROFESSIONAL MILITARY EDUCATION
IN THE U.S. DEPARTMENT OF DEFENSE

CHARLES A. GOLDMAN, PAUL W. MAYBERRY, NATHAN THOMPSON,
TRAVIS HUBBLE, KATHERYN GIGLIO

For more information on this publication, visit **www.rand.org/t/RRA1694-1**.

About RAND

The RAND Corporation is a research organization that develops solutions to public policy challenges to help make communities throughout the world safer and more secure, healthier and more prosperous. RAND is nonprofit, nonpartisan, and committed to the public interest. To learn more about RAND, visit www.rand.org.

Research Integrity

Our mission to help improve policy and decisionmaking through research and analysis is enabled through our core values of quality and objectivity and our unwavering commitment to the highest level of integrity and ethical behavior. To help ensure our research and analysis are rigorous, objective, and nonpartisan, we subject our research publications to a robust and exacting quality-assurance process; avoid both the appearance and reality of financial and other conflicts of interest through staff training, project screening, and a policy of mandatory disclosure; and pursue transparency in our research engagements through our commitment to the open publication of our research findings and recommendations, disclosure of the source of funding of published research, and policies to ensure intellectual independence. For more information, visit www.rand.org/about/research-integrity.

RAND's publications do not necessarily reflect the opinions of its research clients and sponsors.

Published by the RAND Corporation, Santa Monica, Calif.
© 2024 RAND Corporation
RAND® is a registered trademark.

Library of Congress Cataloging-in-Publication Data is available for this publication.
ISBN: 978-1-9774-1117-4

Front Cover: U.S. Air National Guard photo/Master Sgt Mike R. Smith; Back cover, top to bottom: Darius Hutton via USAF, Kathy Reesey, Master Sgt. William Wiseman, R.J. Oriez
Design: Rick Penn-Kraus

Limited Print and Electronic Distribution Rights

Summary

Educated, trained, and experienced military officers enable the Department of Defense (DoD) to accomplish its missions at home and abroad. All military services emphasize education as part of officer development. However, the effectiveness of officer professional military education (PME) has been questioned for the past 30 years. Concerns include the inadequacy of accountability, jointness, and responsiveness to ever-evolving DoD priorities.

To gain a clearer understanding of the state of PME, Congress asked DoD to develop a broad overview of the officer PME system in Section 576 of the 2021 National Defense Authorization Act. The Office of Force Education and Training within the Office of the Under Secretary of Defense for Personnel and Readiness in turn asked RAND National Security Research Institute (NDRI) researchers to aid in fulfilling this request. Specifically, the RAND NDRI team was asked to

1. describe the DoD education system
2. review the ways the system operates, how it compares with civilian institutions, and how it interacts with service talent management
3. analyze the effects of potential changes to DoD, service, and institution policies and practices
4. identify opportunities where the system can be better aligned to DoD's needs.

The RAND team approached these objectives by first developing an analytic framework that encapsulated the policies, processes, and outcomes of the sizable PME system. Data were gathered from three sources: educational institutions directly involved with PME, discussions with representatives of the institutions and talent management experts from the services, and case studies of five comparable civilian educational institutions that offer professional master's degree programs. These data collections were carefully evaluated to respond to the four objectives above.

This study focused on the types of education available to officers at the intermediate and senior levels (generally grades O-4 through O-6). The types of officer education, the institutions that offer them, and the degrees or certificates that the officers earn that were included in the study are shown in Table S.1. In the study, we classified military education institutions as *strategic/operational* (divided into intermediate and senior levels) or *technical*, as shown in the table.

TABLE S.1

Types of Education, Educational Institutions, and Degree Programs Included in This Study

TYPE AND SCHOOL	PARENT INSTITUTION	DEGREE PROGRAM(S)
Intermediate PME offering Joint Professional Military Education, Phase I (JPME-I) credit		
Air Command and Staff College	Air University	Master of Military Operational Art and Science
Army Command and General Staff College	Army University	Master of Military Art and Science; Master of Operational Studies
Marine Corps Command and Staff College	Marine Corps University	Master of Military Studies
College of Naval Command and Staff	Naval War College	Master of Defense and Strategic Studies
Senior PME offering Joint Professional Military Education, Phase II (JPME-II) credit		
Air War College	Air University	Master of Strategic Studies
Army War College	n/a	Master of Strategic Studies
Marine Corps War College	Marine Corps University	Master of Strategic Studies
College of Naval Warfare	Naval War College	Master of National Security and Strategic Studies
Joint and Combined Warfighting School	National Defense University (NDU) (Joint Forces Staff College)	Non-degree
Joint Advanced Warfighting School	NDU (Joint Forces Staff College)	Master of Joint Campaign Planning and Strategy
National War College	NDU	Master of National Security Studies
Eisenhower School for National Security and Resource Strategy	NDU	Master of National Security Resource Strategy
College of International Security Affairs	NDU	Master of Strategic Security Studies; Master of Joint Special Operations
College of Information and Cyberspace	NDU	Master of Government Information Leadership
Technical Schools		
Air Force Institute of Technology	Air University	27 master's degrees and 14 Ph.D.s in STEM-related programs
U.S. Army Armament Graduate School	U.S. Army Combat Capabilities Development Command–Armaments Center	Ph.D. in armament engineering
Joint Special Operations University	U.S. Special Operations Command	[No degrees]
Naval Postgraduate School	n/a	83 master's degrees and 15 Ph.D.s in STEM-related, management, and international studies programs

SOURCE: Information supplied by educational institutions.

NOTE: n/a = not applicable. STEM = science, technology, engineering, and math.

Findings and Opportunities

The military educational institutions share many features with civilian institutions in terms of how they admit and graduate students, the methods they use for teaching, and the ways they manage their faculty. But there are important differences. Civilian institutions operate in wide-ranging markets with students coming to them from many sources and taking jobs across a large range of employers. The military institutions, by contrast, operate within the specific personnel development system of DoD and its services. Summarized here are main findings from the study that address those areas Congress expressed interest in. For some, but not all, areas of findings, we offer opportunities that DoD can consider for enhancing the overall PME system.

Educational Standards

All military educational institutions in the study are accredited by civilian agencies. Strategic/operational-focused programs are also accredited by the Chairman of the Joint Chiefs of Staff (CJCS). Although there is no CJCS or Office of the Secretary of Defense (OSD) requirement for PME programs to be accredited by civilian higher-education agencies, all service intermediate and senior-level PME programs examined in the study have been accredited by their regional academic accrediting bodies. This means that they possess sufficiently rigorous academic quality to award graduate degrees. The CJCS administers NDU and accredits each of the PME programs that provide Joint Professional Military Education (JPME) credentials but does not run or direct them. The individual services and OSD oversee PME offered at the service educational institutions, with input from the educational institutions, the service and joint operational needs and priorities, the priorities and policies articulated by the CJCS, and congressional requirements.

Educational standards and practices remain a challenge. The most recent CJCS accreditation review, in 2020, found that all service intermediate and senior-level PME programs met or partially met all seven educational standard requirements. These standards relate to joint awareness, instructional methods, program assessment, faculty practices, student assessments, and resources. Only three of the eight PME programs met all seven requirements, and only two of the seven requirements were met by all programs, with the most common deficiency being in faculty recruitment, selection, assignment, and performance assessment.

Talent Management, Admissions, and Graduation

Student admission processes vary greatly between civilian and military educational institutions. Civilian programs apply their own admissions standards and dedicate significant resources to recruiting and selecting their students. Military education institutions operate to serve the services' talent management processes and are, therefore, not resourced to conduct student admissions. The technical military education institutions do review candidates to determine whether learners are prepared to undertake rigorous technical studies (as civilian institutions do). In interviews, the services did not express a need to change these approaches.

Commitment to student graduation is key to both military and civilian education institutions. Both the military schools and a set of civilian schools we assessed in the study graduate the vast majority of their students. All institutions offer similar and significant academic support programs to students who are not on track to meet graduation requirements. There is little interest in changing these practices, according to study-related interviews and discussions.

Military educational institutions want more outcomes-based information to inform planning. The outcomes-based military education adopted in the recent Joint Chiefs of Staff (JCS) Vision calls for decisions on curricula and teaching methods to be informed by graduate outcomes.[1] Military schools participating in this study expressed strong support for this vision. However, interviewees noted that their schools face significant challenges in getting actionable information from the services and joint community to help them make these decisions.

Opportunity: Develop better signals of demand and value from the services and joint community to inform school curriculum decisions relative to expected outcomes required of graduates. This can help to offset the challenges in getting actionable information from the services and joint community to make curricula and teaching method decisions based on education outcomes.

Services and schools report that postgraduation assignments often do not build on the skills learned during officer PME experiences. A 2021 RAND study also found that this divergence is a source of frustration for military students.[2] Some communities are capitalizing on PME experiences in graduate assignments, however. Such connections tend to be from technical schools or higher-level strategy programs (e.g., the Joint Advanced Warfighting School and similar service schools). Seeking to better integrate PME and talent management is an area of emphasis in the JCS Vision Statement.

Opportunity: Build on service talent management efforts in specialized areas that have had success in matching PME graduates' experience and educational outcomes to assignment opportunities. Although many services and schools repeatedly reported that postgraduation assignments do not build on PME education and skills, there are some success stories. An examination of what these schools are doing right may help inform the services' utilization of talent management going forward.

---

[1]   Joint Chiefs of Staff, *Developing Today's Joint Officers for Tomorrow's Ways of War: The Joint Chiefs of Staff Vision and Guidance for Professional Military Education and Talent Management,* May 1, 2020.

[2]   Paul W. Mayberry, Charles A. Goldman, Kimberly Jackson, Eric Hastings, Hannah Acheson-Field, and Anthony Lawrence, *Making the Grade: Integration of Joint Professional Military Education and Talent Management in Developing Joint Officers,* RAND Corporation, RR-A473-1, 2021.

Faculty Management and the Role of Research

Military education institutions approach civilian faculty tenure in different ways. Like civilian institutions, some offer civilian faculty tenure; others appoint civilians to renewable terms. Conversations that we had with military educational staff suggested that a recurring appointment ("tenure without tenure") is the standard outcome for renewable contracts, so long as an instructor continues to perform well in the classroom and the institution continues to require teaching in the instructor's areas of expertise. Some interviewees expressed that this model is an effective means of maintaining institutional quality, as well as the flexibility necessary to offer officers up-to-date insight on complex challenges.

The use of adjunct faculty varies across military education institutions. Some schools in the study depend on only a small number of adjunct faculty because they prefer those faculty members who are full-time and thus more likely to be tightly connected to the institution. Other schools, such as the U.S. Army Armament Graduate School, rely primarily on adjunct faculty to teach the bulk of the courses. Interviewees at adjunct-heavy schools thought that adjuncts provided the flexibility to bring in the kinds of specialized expertise and knowledge that may be needed at a particular time.

Opportunity: Explore additional opportunities for adjunct and visiting faculty. While some institutions depend on such faculty members, others expressed no interest in bringing on those who do not have strong ties to their institutions. However, adjunct and visiting faculty can bring expertise in specific fields and topics and may also have valuable relationships with other components and agencies. Such faculty could help institutions address changing topics, such as the Chairman's Special Areas of Emphasis,[3] and broaden institutions' connections with the services and other DoD agencies in other ways.

Faculty and student research is valued as an important part of professional development in military education institutions. Over the course of the study, both faculty and administrators noted that the relationship between teaching and research is synergistic. Often, research efforts ensured that contemporary materials were incorporated into instruction. Moreover, interviewees noted how student officers can hone critical thinking and analytical skills through their own research initiatives. We did not observe any adverse effects associated with the balance between teaching and research commitments.

Serving as faculty may not be seen as career enhancing for officers. Military educational institutions typically are seeking high-quality officers for their respective faculty. Representatives of military schools generally think that, over the past several years, services have not valued teaching positions as career enhancing (and individual officers

---

[3] See Joseph F. Dunford, Jr., "Special Areas of Emphasis for Joint Professional Military Education in Academic Years 2020 and 2021," memorandum for the chiefs of the military services and the President, National Defense University, CM-0108-19, May 6, 2019.

may share this perception). This perception may be compounded because officers currently cannot receive joint credit experience (which is a requirement for selection to general or flag officer) for teaching at their own service institutions, although they do receive it when teaching at another service or joint institution.

Opportunity: Consider granting joint assignment credit for military faculty at senior institutions, even within the faculty members' own services, to promote the value of faculty assignments.

Officer Class Sizes and Program Alternatives

There is no broad indication of need for or interest in increasing or decreasing the number of officers attending PME. The general perception of interviewees was that the military education system produces enough graduates to address service and joint needs. However, this issue has not been systematically studied by the services.

Navy officials noted feeling compelled to feed officers into the JPME system despite the need for them to conduct Navy operations. The JPME system requires the participation of a mix of officers from every service. However, Navy interviewees noted that their service could use their officers more efficiently by sending fewer of them to JPME and reserving more of them for operational naval assignments. Because of the statutory requirements for a mix of joint representation in both the student body and the faculty, Navy interviewees said that it is consistently difficult to satisfy both the service and joint requirements for educated and experienced officers.

Civilian academic institutions can support aspects of officer education but, without adjustments, will not meet PME needs. Congress asked whether students could attend civilian institutions instead of PME institutions. Certainly, many officers do attend civilian graduate programs, and these experiences can play valuable roles in officer development. However, civilian offerings cannot devote the requisite attention to federal and DoD policy and strategy that officers require in their military leadership roles. Similarly, civilian programs generally do not satisfy JPME requirements that are needed for any officers to be considered for promotion to flag or general officer, although the U.S. Space Force is currently pursuing a combined civilian-military program that meets JPME requirements. Working with the JPME oversight organizations, the service is seeking to comply with the requisite congressional and policy requirements to ensure that civilian offerings and their graduates will be designated as joint qualified. The U.S. Space Force innovation offers a valuable opportunity to monitor, assess, and determine whether it holds lessons that can be applied more broadly. Accordingly, formative and summative evaluations should be an explicit design feature of the program. Such evaluations can inform future decisions on whether some of the present demand met by military educational institutions could realistically be met by civilian institutions, with or without relief from congressional statutes or joint policy requirements.

Conclusion

Congress asked fundamental questions regarding the role, conduct, and management of PME in DoD. In our research, the services largely expressed satisfaction with the alignment of military educational institutions with their mission needs, although the Navy would prefer to lighten the involvement of its officers in JPME. The Joint Staff also raised concerns, calling for PME institutions to increase their classified capabilities and facilities to support evolving joint operational concepts. We found that technical institutions naturally focus on more technical content and have a more direct style of instruction. In contrast, strategic/operational institutions cover broader topics with more use of techniques, such as case studies, that allow students to appreciate complex interactions, past lessons, and applications to future uncertainties. Technical institutions have important input into student selection, and their graduates often are placed into relevant follow-on assignments. Strategic/operational institutions, on the other hand, receive students selected by the services to meet talent management goals, and the relation of follow-on assignments can be unclear.

We identified several opportunities for enhancing the DoD educational system and its supporting processes. The schools and services would benefit from clearer expressions of demand that schools can use to guide development of curricula and adoption of teaching methods. The services can build on existing talent management efforts in specialized areas by increasing the overall match between PME graduates' educational outcomes and subsequent assignment opportunities. Although we found that some schools use a variety of adjunct and visiting faculty, others show little or no use of these options. We think all schools should assess their opportunities to use such faculty to expand their educational capabilities and stakeholder networks in support of meeting mission demands.

Chapter 6 of the report provides a specific response to each issue that Congress raised in Section 576. All responses are based on the analyses summarized above.

Contents

Tables, Figures, and Boxes

Figures

Boxes

CHAPTER 1

Introduction

Educated, trained, and experienced military officers enable the Department of Defense (DoD) to accomplish its missions at home and across the world. All service branches emphasize education as part of officer development. However, the effectiveness of officer professional military education (PME) has been questioned for the past 30 years. Concerns include the inadequacy of accountability, jointness, and responsiveness to ever-evolving DoD priorities.[1]

Over the past few years, DoD, the Joint Chiefs of Staff (JCS), and the services have made changes in policy and guidance that are intended to improve the way the officer education system functions. In 2020, for example, the JCS articulated their vision for PME in their May 2020 publication, *Developing Today's Joint Officers for Tomorrow's Ways of War: The Joint Chiefs of Staff Vision and Guidance for Professional Military Education and Talent Management.*[2] At the same time, the Chairman of the Joint Chiefs of Staff (CJCS) issued a revised version of the Officer Professional Military Education Policy (OPMEP).[3] Both documents mandate an outcomes-based strategy to guide PME, with information on the needs of the services and the performance of graduates used to develop the learning objectives, curricula, and teaching methods used by DoD's educational institutions.

In support of these objectives, in April 2022, DoD issued its first instruction on PME, *Military Education: Program Management and Administration.*[4] This instruction establishes accountabilities for outcomes-based education and directs the synchronization of military education policy with Talent Management—that is, how faculty are assigned to teach PME and how officers are selected to enroll in PME and utilized upon graduating across all joint and service educational institutions.

Despite this progress, it is difficult to evaluate attempts to adapt DoD's educational institutions in response to higher direction or to mea-

---

[1] U.S. House of Representatives Committee on Armed Services, *Report of the Panel on Military Education,* 101st Congress, April 21, 1989; Jim Mattis, *Summary of the 2018 National Defense Strategy of the United States of America: Sharpening the American Military's Competitive Edge,* U.S. Department of Defense, January 2018.

[2] Joint Chiefs of Staff, *Developing Today's Joint Officers for Tomorrow's Ways of War: The Joint Chiefs of Staff Vision and Guidance for Professional Military Education and Talent Management,* May 1, 2020.

[3] Chairman of the Joint Chiefs of Staff Instruction 1800.01F, *Officer Professional Military Education Policy,* May 15, 2020.

[4] Department of Defense Instruction (DoDI) 1322.35, *Military Education: Program Management and Administration,* Vol. 1, April 26, 2022.

sure the system's effectiveness in a context in which programs must compete for scarce resources. There is a need for a detailed understanding of the entire enterprise, including a baseline assessment of supply, demand, and effectiveness. Along with other stakeholders, Congress has periodically raised questions about the components of the officer education system, their functions, and their relationship to other elements of DoD. In Section 576 of the Fiscal Year (FY) 2021 National Defense Authorization Act (NDAA),[5] Congress asked DoD to prepare a study of the officer PME system, including a factual overview, an assessment of certain aspects of the system, and an analysis of certain potential changes to the system.

The Office of Force Education and Training within the Office of the Under Secretary of Defense for Personnel and Readiness (OUSD[P&R]) asked researchers from the RAND National Defense Research Institute (NDRI) to aid in fulfilling this request by preparing a response to the congressional request. Specifically, we were asked to assist in fulfilling four broad objectives:

1. Describe the DoD education system factually.
2. Review the ways the system operates, how it compares with civilian institutions, and how it interacts with service talent management.
3. Analyze effects of potential changes to DoD, service, and institution policies and practices.
4. Identify opportunities where the system can be better aligned to DoD's needs.

Study Scope and Approach

The education of U.S. military officers starts before commissioning and extends throughout an officer's career. Both officers and enlisted members participate in various forms of PME. Table 1.1 offers an overview of officer PME levels. This report focuses on institutions that officers typically attend during the intermediate and senior levels of their careers (in the darker shaded rows). As shown in the table, institutions at the three highest levels award Joint Professional Military Education (JPME) credit.

Types of Officer Education Examined

The first objective of the study, as guided by Section 576, required us to collect information about individual DoD educational institutions. In all, we reviewed 13 institutions (listed in the first row of Table 1.2). Together, the 13 selected institutions offer intermediate and senior officer education. These types of education are referred to throughout this report and are described at further length in Chapter 2. In later chapters, we present key findings using a format similar to the one used in this table.

---

[5]   Public Law 116-283, William M. (Mac) Thornberry National Defense Authorization Act for Fiscal Year 2021, January 1, 2021, Section 576, "Report on Potential Improvements to Certain Military Educational Institutions of the Department of Defense."

TABLE 1.1

Overview of Officer PME

LEVEL	GRADE	JPME CREDIT
Pre-commissioning	Before O-1	None
Primary	O-1–O-3	None
Intermediate	O-4	JPME-I
Senior	O-5–O-6	JPME-II
General/flag officer	O-7+	CAPSTONE

NOTE: JPME-I = Joint Professional Military Education, Phase I. JPME-II = Joint Professional Military Education, Phase II.

TABLE 1.2

Educational Institutions Reviewed in This Report

	STRATEGIC/OPERATIONAL	TECHNICAL
Military	Intermediate level • Air Command and Staff College (ACSC) • Army Command and General Staff College • Marine Corps Command and Staff College (CSC) • College of Naval Command and Staff (CNC&S) Senior level • Air War College (AWC) • U.S. Army War College (USAWC) • Marine Corps War College (MCWAR) • College of Naval Warfare (CNW) • National Defense University (NDU)	• Air Force Institute of Technology (AFIT) • U.S. Army Armament Graduate School (AGS) • Joint Special Operations University (JSOU) • Naval Postgraduate School (NPS)
Civilian	• Johns Hopkins University School of Advanced International Studies (JHU SAIS), Master of Arts in International Affairs • George Washington University, School of Business, Master of Business Administration • Arizona State University, School of Public Affairs, Master of Public Administration	• University of Maryland, Master of Engineering in Cybersecurity • Purdue University, Krannert School of Management, Master of Science in Global Supply Chain Management

JPME. As Table 1.1 shows, JPME credit is awarded in three phases corresponding to the three highest levels of military education. Once an officer reaches or is selected for field-grade or mid-grade rank (O-4), they typically become eligible for the JPME system, which addresses both joint and service-specific training and education needs. Service command and staff schools and a joint option at the National Intelligence University (not studied in this report) offer intermediate-level programs in JPME-I, typically to officers in the grade of O-4 (major or lieutenant commander). Service war colleges and multiple joint colleges at NDU offer senior-level programs in JPME-II, typically to officers in the grades of O-5 and O-6. The third phase of PME is offered only through NDU's CAPSTONE course to general and flag officers. JPME, in general, provides the education needed to develop service officers to be proficient in joint matters (as defined in 10 U.S.C. § 668).[6]

Strategic/operational education. In Section 576, Congress asked that this study include all service institutions that operate at the intermediate and senior levels and NDU, which operates at the intermediate, senior, and general/flag officer levels. We use the term *strategic/operational-focused* to refer to the intermediate-level institutions, which focus on the operational level of warfighting, and the senior-level institutions, which focus on the strategic level of warfighting. Table 1.2 shows the nine military strategic/operational-focused institutions included in this report.

Technical education. DoD maintains specialized institutions that offer graduate degrees and certificates or other forms of learning in specific technical fields of study. Congress specifically asked that three of these institutions be included in this study: AFIT, AGS, and JSOU. Congress allowed the Secretary of Defense to designate additional institutions, and the Secretary designated NPS, which is also a specialized institution at a similar level. These four institutions do not line up completely with the levels shown in Table 1.1, but officers typically attend these institutions at the intermediate stage, either instead of attending an institution that grants JPME-I credit or in addition to attending one of those institutions. These institutions also maintain arrangements for officers to receive JPME-I credit, either in person or through distance learning, if they have not already received it. JSOU is different from the other institutions included in this study because its mission is to offer only relatively short continuing education and professional development, rather than graduate degree programs.

Civilian educational institutions. Military and DoD civilian personnel can access education at civilian institutions through fellowship and continuing education programs. In these, officers can enroll as full- or part-time students. Congress asked several questions about how DoD's educational institutions compare with civilian institutions and whether civilian institutions could serve some of the needs presently met by

---

[6] This material is adapted from Paul W. Mayberry, Charles A. Goldman, Kimberly Jackson, Eric Hastings, Hannah Acheson-Field, and Anthony Lawrence, *Making the Grade: Integration of Joint Professional Military Education and Talent Management in Developing Joint Officers*, RAND Corporation, RR-A473-1, 2021, drawing on Chairman of the Joint Chiefs of Staff Instruction 1800.01F, 2020.

military educational institutions. To respond to Congress's questions, we collaborated with our sponsor to select five civilian professional master's degree programs for case studies. We consider these programs comparable to the DoD institutions because they offer master's degrees in somewhat equivalent professional fields of study. The five civilian programs are listed in the second row of Table 1.2. They are distributed across different fields of study that a mid-career military officer might reasonably undertake. We sought civilian institutions that reflected the two distinct groupings of the military PME schools: three institutions with a more strategic content orientation and two with a more technical content orientation.

Types of Policies and Practices Evaluated

In addition to factually documenting the officer education enterprise (research objective 1), we were asked to conduct evaluations and analyses of the effects of potential changes to specified DoD, service, and institution policies and practices (research objectives 2 and 3). Box 1.1 presents the research topics requested in Section 576 and addressed in this study.

We considered these topics, as well as concerns raised in other reports that consider the ways that DoD and institutions of higher education operate. All of these are discussed in subsequent chapters of this report.

Analytic Framework

This study involved a wide range of topics, as outlined in the congressional language of Box 1.1. We developed a general framework to organize these topics and to guide our analysis. This framework, depicted in Figure 1.1, categorizes the many topics into four general areas:

- fundamental *service and joint requirements* for graduates and other educational products and services
- *inputs* provided by the military services in the form of officers to be students and faculty, along with sufficient resources allowing institutions to achieve their respective missions
- formalized and systematic *processes* by which the educational systems operate
- *outcomes* resulting from the educational enterprise's investment of resources via systematic processes to address the expected requirements.

A final factor of this framework involves the communication and feedback mechanisms needed to ensure effective and efficient alignment among the system components and to serve as the basis for continuous process improvement. In addition to capturing logic model elements, the framework encapsulates the interactions among educational institutions and the services' talent management systems that were discussed in an earlier RAND NDRI study.[7] As detailed in the

---

[7] Mayberry et al., 2021.

BOX 1.1

Topics Listed in Section 576 of 2021 NDAA

1. Review and assess the potential effects of the following actions on the military education provided by the 13 DoD educational institutions:

   a. Modification of admission and graduation requirements.

   b. Expansion of use of case studies in curricula for professional military education.

   c. Reduction or expansion of degree-granting authority.

   d. Reduction or expansion of the acceptance of research grants.

   e. Reduction or expansion of the number of attending students generally.

   f. Modification of military personnel career milestones in order to prioritize instructor positions.

   g. Increase in educational and performance requirements for military personnel selected to be instructors.

   h. Expansion of visiting or adjunct faculty.

   i. Modification of civilian faculty management practices, including employment practices.

   j. Reduction of the number of attending students through the sponsoring of education of an increased number of students at non–Department of Defense institutions of higher education.

2. Assess the differences between admission standards and graduation requirements of the 13 DoD educational institutions and such admission standards and graduation requirements of comparable civilian schools.

3. Assess the requirements of the goals and missions of the 13 DoD educational institutions and any need to adjust such goals and missions to meet national security requirements of DoD.

4. Assess the effectiveness and shortfalls of the existing professional military education enterprise as measured against graduate utilization, postgraduate evaluations, and the education and force development requirements of the Chairman of the Joint Chiefs of Staff and the Chiefs of the Armed Forces.

SOURCE: Adapted from Public Law 116-283, William M. (Mac) Thornberry National Defense Authorization Act for Fiscal Year 2021, January 1, 2021, Section 576, "Report on Potential Improvements to Certain Military Educational Institutions of the Department of Defense."

next section, we used this framework to organize the remainder of this report, although we do not explicitly address in detail the issue of requirements.

Information for each element in the framework came from a variety of sources:

Institutional information. Our sponsor in OUSD(P&R) fielded three requests for information. Two of these were directed to the DoD educational institutions. The first asked for factual information about programs, students, faculty, and staff of the 13 military education

FIGURE 1.1

Study Framework for Officer PME

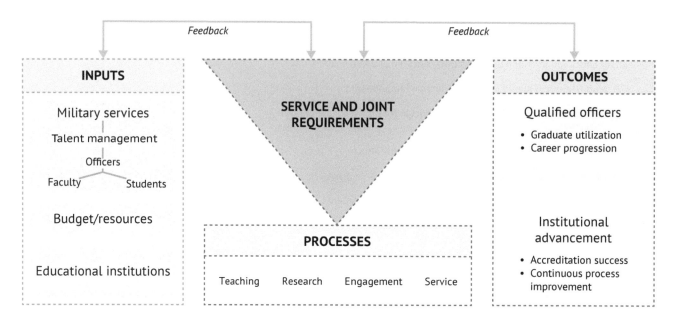

institutions. The second asked the institutions to explain their processes in greater detail and consider the effects of potential changes to policies or practices. The third request was made to the military services, asking them to explain practices for talent management and military faculty selection. That request also asked the services to provide information about how graduates are utilized.

Stakeholder discussions. We followed these requests with a group discussion with each educational institution, each service talent management community, and the Joint Staff (J-7, Joint Force Development). These discussions served to clarify the written responses and explore related topics in greater depth.

Civilian institution case studies. In addition to these efforts within DoD, we examined five selected civilian institution programs (listed in the second row of Table 1.2). To conduct these case studies, we met with representatives of each of the programs in one group discussion for each program. We also reviewed the program websites and additional written information the programs provided. These case studies addressed topics related to the inputs, processes, outputs, and outcomes of each program.

We analyzed this information by conducting a thematic review of the military educational institutions, military services, and civilian case studies that was organized according to the elements depicted in Figure 1.1, which allowed us to address the topics raised by Congress.

Organization of This Report

The next chapter offers a larger overview of the PME system, with special attention given to the institutions examined in this study. The subsequent chapters are guided by the analytic framework (Figure 1.1), as it captures the many working parts of the PME system. Chapter 3 examines the *inputs* to the system—that is, its oversight by the Office of the Secretary of Defense (OSD) and the services, officer admission into the PME system, and how the system is resourced. Chapter 4 investigates the *processes* by which officers are educated in PME. Here, we review the processes related to teaching, research, engagement, and service. Chapter 5 presents our findings pertaining to the intended PME system *outcomes*: producing qualified officers and developing institutions designed specifically to educate and train qualified officers. Chapter 6 synthesizes the findings of the study and responds to the specific topics Congress raised. This chapter also discusses opportunities for system enhancement, based on our evaluation of the PME system and civilian institutions. They are not recommendations per se. Instead, they are designed to offer OSD, the services, and military educational institutions ideas to consider as they continue to enhance and improve parts of the PME system going forward.

This analysis is supported by detailed factual profiles of each military educational institution reviewed in this study, which are provided in the appendix.

CHAPTER 2

Overview of the PME System

Military education develops officers and enlisted military members so that they can function effectively in their duties. PME is a subset of military education that prepares service members for increasing levels of responsibilities and eventual joint leadership responsibilities.[1] Strategic/operational PME "conveys the broad body of knowledge and develops the habits of mind [that are] essential to the military professional's expertise in the art and science of war."[2] It typically includes education in such areas as military history, ethics, the profession of arms, critical thinking, communication, problem-solving, and leadership.[3] Strategic/operational PME is distinguished from the technical education provided for specific duties and career fields. It is also different from the education offered in civilian graduate schools. Here, we describe officer education both broadly and in the contexts of technical education and graduate studies.

PME Offering JPME Credit

As shown in Chapter 1 (Table 1.1), officer education, including PME, begins prior to commissioning and continues throughout the officer's career. Prior to commissioning, officer PME typically occurs in conjunction with a traditional undergraduate education through service academies or Reserve Officers' Training Corps (ROTC) programs at colleges and universities. For those officers who commission outside an academy or ROTC, pre-commissioning PME occurs in an officer training or officer candidate school.

After commissioning, company- and junior-grade officers (O-1 to O-3) typically attend primary developmental PME in at least one in-residence course lasting anywhere from five to 20 weeks. This PME focuses on primary skill building and basic leadership training and may be tailored to an officer's career field. Once an officer achieves or is selected for O-4, the officer typically becomes eligible for intermediate-level PME. Intermediate-level PME develops officers for senior

---

[1] DoDI 1322.35, 2022, glossary.

[2] DoDI 1322.35, 2022, glossary.

[3] DoDI 1322.35, 2022, glossary and 4.1(a).

operational-level duties. This is the first level of PME offering joint credit (JPME).

JPME, established under the Goldwater-Nichols Act, is focused on educating officers in joint matters. According to the 1994 NDAA,

> "[T]he primary mission of the joint professional military education schools is to provide military officers with expertise in the integrated employment of land, sea, and air forces, including matters relating to national security strategy, national military strategy, strategic planning and contingency planning, and command and control of combat operations under unified command."[4]

JPME credit is required for some joint duty assignments and for an officer to be joint qualified, which is an eligibility requirement for certain positions and promotions, including promotion to the general/flag officer level (O-7).

Intermediate-level PME offering JPME-I credit is mostly delivered through the four service command and staff colleges and National Intelligence University (NIU) using in-residence, distance learning, and hybrid delivery modes. In-residence programs typically last one academic year and offer a master's degree. NIU's JPME program offers both PME and technical education, including two master's degrees in intelligence. NIU is not studied in this report.

Officers in the rank of O-5 and O-6 may be eligible to attend senior-level PME offering JPME-II credit. Senior-level PME educates senior officers for strategic duties. This PME is offered in the four service war colleges and five NDU institutions that offer six PME programs. The six PME programs at NDU each have a unique focus, such as national resource strategy, cyberspace, and international security affairs. Except for the NDU's Joint and Combined Warfighting School (JCWS), which follows a ten-week schedule, all programs are ten-month in-residence programs and offer master's degrees.

In addition to curricular requirements, discussed further in Chapter 3, schools offering JPME credit must have a mix of officers from each service plus relevant U.S. government civilians.[5] They sometimes also enroll American defense industry representatives and international military officers.

Each school offering PME has a particular emphasis that might best position its graduates for certain assignments. For example, students at the College of Information and Cyberspace (CIC), within NDU, are anticipated to be more effective than students at other schools in positions focused on cyberspace. Each service's war college PME program offering JPME credit has a particular emphasis on the domain of that service (e.g., air, land, sea) but is designed for, and required to have, a diverse student population that includes members of all the services.

---

4   National Defense Authorization Act for Fiscal Year 1994, Public Law 103-160, November 30, 1993, Section 921.

5   Chairman of the Joint Chiefs of Staff Instruction 1800.01F, 2020, Enclosure A, 9.b.

While JPME-II credit is overwhelmingly offered in residence, many JPME-I programs have remote learning options. Most of these options provide flexibility, allowing the service member to complete the education while performing other duties over a longer period. Most remote learning options do not confer a master's degree, though some have this option.

At the time of this study, the PME needs of the U.S. Space Force officer corps were initially to be met by Air University (AU). However, in October 2022, the Chief of Space Operations broke from tradition by announcing that the Space Force would partner with JHU SAIS to provide independent, residential intermediate and senior development educational offerings.[6] The program is nascent and is to be implemented in 2023, with final details and issues still being resolved. Accordingly, we cannot comment on the veracity of the concept but do view the approach as one that is worthy of merit and that should be

---

[6] Secretary of the Air Force Public Affairs, "Space Force to Partner with Johns Hopkins University SAIS for Service-Specific IDE, SDE," *Space Force News*, October 26, 2022.

properly evaluated and examined for implications for other military educational offerings.

Technical Education

Technical military education for specific officer career fields is typically offered through both primary and continuing education programs. Technical education programs are most often provided through military education institutions because such programs concentrate on military-specific applications of technical knowledge. However, fellowships or other sponsorship programs at civilian institutions are also viable options for officers. Most military technical education offers certificates and/or licensing. Examples include flight school; special operations instruction; and various specialized cyber, engineering, and health sciences programs. Some military technical education programs provide advanced degrees. In addition to those technical schools studied in this report (listed in Table 2.1), other military education institutions that provide advanced degrees include the Uniformed Services University of the Health Sciences in Bethesda, Maryland, which offers a medical degree (M.D.) and 21 other health-related advanced degrees; the Army Judge Advocate General's Legal Center and School in Charlottesville, Virginia, which offers a master of laws (L.L.M.) degree; and the National Intelligence University in Fort Meade, Maryland, which offers two master's degrees in intelligence, along with JPME-I credit. CIC, within NDU, which is included in our study, provides both JPME-II credit and technical education.

Technical military education also includes several non-degree programs related to specific career fields. In this report, we present data on only one, JSOU, located at MacDill Air Force Base in Tampa, Florida, which provides technical programs to enlisted members and officers engaged in special operations.

Overview of Institutions Included in This Report

A list of the PME institutions studied in this report, and the programs they offer, is in Table 2.1. The table organizes the included strategic/operational PME programs by the level of JPME credit offered and also includes the technical schools. The table includes several indicators of institutional size. Although NDU includes multiple colleges, each with a unique focus and degree offered, these indicators of institutional size cannot be clearly divided among its multiple programs and are thus aggregated.

Many of the institutions offer residential, distance learning, and hybrid learning options, all of which are reviewed in this report. Comparing measurements for distance and hybrid learning programs with measurements for residential programs can be complex. For instance, students may be enrolled without making significant progress in some distance learning programs for multiple years, and faculty utilization for distance learning varies significantly. To offer a straightforward comparison of program sizes, only residential programs are reflected in Table 2.1. With the exception of JSOU, which does not offer degrees, the data for enrolled students in the table include only those students enrolled in programs leading to degrees.

In addition to the programs listed in the table, NDU and the service command and staff colleges operate advanced strategic programs, which typically follow completion of JPME-I. These programs are operated by the Joint Advanced Warfighting School (JAWS), the School of Advanced Military Studies (SAMS), the School of Advanced Air and Space Studies (SAASS), the Maritime Advanced Warfighting School (MAWS), and the School of Advanced Warfighting (SAW).

As the notes in the table indicate, the Army's SAMS also offers a more advanced JPME-II program. Because the indicators for this JPME-II program cannot be disaggregated from the larger Army Command and General Staff College, it is not reflected in the list of programs offering JPME-II credit.

More-complete information about each institution, including students enrolled in distance and hybrid learning, is available in the appendix.

Civilian Education

The U.S. military permits a significant number of officers to obtain graduate degrees at civilian institutions. These opportunities include (1) non-sponsored opportunities for service members to take extended leave to obtain an advanced degree at their own cost and (2) sponsored fellowship opportunities for service members to attend a civilian school while remaining active duty and receiving pay. Fellowship programs include degrees and programs in various technical fields, such as medical, legal, and science, technology, engineering, and math—related (STEM-related) disciplines, as well as in leadership and public administration fields, such as acquisition, public policy, international relations, and management-related disciplines. Military officers who are sponsored to obtain an advanced degree at a civilian institution are typically assigned to a military educational institution for administrative oversight while attending the civilian school.

Military officers attending civilian institutions typically attend courses with civilians, including international students. While some civilian programs provide education with content similar in part to the programs taught at military educational institutions, they do not provide military-specific strategic/operational and technical education and rely only on unclassified content. Officers do not receive JPME credit for enrollment in civilian education programs.[7]

The U.S. military permits a significant number of officers to obtain graduate degrees at civilian institutions.

---

[7] The U.S. Space Force is working with appropriate defense oversight organizations to ensure that the necessary conditions and standards are achieved by the JHU SAIS PME offerings and graduates so that they can be properly designated as "joint," as defined in published policies and statutes.

TABLE 2.1

Summary of Selected Military Educational Institutions (FY 2022)

TYPE AND SCHOOL	PARENT INSTITUTION	DEGREE PROGRAM	RESIDENTIAL STUDENTS ENROLLED	FACULTY (FTE)	BUDGET ($M)
Intermediate PME offering JPME-I credit					
ACSC	AU	Master of Military Operational Art and Science	511	139	$40.9
Army Command and General Staff College	Army University	Master of Military Art and Science; Master of Operational Studies	1,503[a]	449[d]	$480.7
Marine Corps CSC	Marine Corps University (MCU)	Master of Military Studies	209	44	$8.3
CNC&S	Naval War College (NWC)	Master of Defense and Strategic Studies	285	149[b]	$17.8
Senior PME offering JPME-II credit					
AWC	AU	Master of Strategic Studies	225	82	$23.1
USAWC	n/a	Master of Strategic Studies	378	236	$21.0
MCWAR	MCU	Master of Strategic Studies	32	9	$2.0
CNW	NWC	Master of National Security and Strategic Studies	199	—[b]	$11.6
JCWS	NDU (Joint Forces Staff College [JFSC])	Non-degree	580[e]	—	—
JAWS	NDU (JFSC)	Master of Joint Campaign Planning and Strategy	44	—	—
National War College	NDU	Master of National Security Studies	209	—	—
Eisenhower School for National Security and Resource Strategy	NDU	Master of National Security Resource Strategy	304	—	—
College of International Security Affairs (CISA)	NDU	Master of Strategic Security Studies; Master of Joint Special Operations[g]	106	—	—

Table 2.1—Continued

TYPE AND SCHOOL	PARENT INSTITUTION	DEGREE PROGRAM	RESIDENTIAL STUDENTS ENROLLED	FACULTY (FTE)	BUDGET ($M)
CIC	NDU	Master of Government Information Leadership	49[f]	–	–
(Totals for NDU)				255	$92.6

Technical Schools

TYPE AND SCHOOL	PARENT INSTITUTION	DEGREE PROGRAM	RESIDENTIAL STUDENTS ENROLLED	FACULTY (FTE)	BUDGET ($M)
AFIT	AU	27 master's degrees and 14 Ph.D.s in STEM-related programs	793	371	$101
AGS	U.S. Army Combat Capabilities Development Command—Armaments Center (DEVCOM-AC)	Ph.D. in armament engineering	37	5	$4.3
JSOU	U.S. Special Operations Command (USSOCOM)	[No degrees]	11,468[h]	67	$27.3
NPS	n/a	83 master's degrees and 15 Ph.D.s in STEM-related, management, and international studies programs	2,119	624	$118.2[c]

SOURCE: Information supplied by educational institutions.

NOTE: FTE = full-time equivalent. n/a = not applicable. All faculty FTE counts are rounded to the nearest whole number. Exact figures can be found in the appendix. The U.S. Space Force PME programs offered by JHU SAIS are not included because the concept has yet to be implemented.

[a] An additional 17 students enrolled in the Army Command and General Staff College's 24-month Advanced Strategic Leader Studies Program within SAMS. Students receive a master of strategic studies, and U.S. military officers also receive JPME-II credit.

[b] The Navy War College employs the same faculty for the Command and Naval Staff College and CNW. The reported faculty for the Command and Naval Staff College includes those who also teach at CNW.

[c] NPS received an additional $106.9 million in reimbursable funding in FY 2022. More details are available in the appendix.

[d] Only resident faculty are included for the Army Command and General Staff College. There are an additional 142 non-resident faculty.

[e] JCWS students in the hybrid delivery option for this course are not included in Table 2.1. Data for hybrid delivery are in the appendix.

[f] Only the residential M.S. program is included. A remotely delivered version of this course, which does not offer JPME credit, is included in the appendix.

[g] CISA operates two M.A. programs, but one (Joint Special Operations) does not offer JPME-II credit.

[h] JSOU numbers reflect total enrollment, inclusive of distance learning programs.

CHAPTER 3

Inputs to PME: The Services, Resources, and Institutions

PME that provides joint credit (JPME) must be responsive to the joint warfighting needs of the military. For that reason, it has been largely overseen by the CJCS, which accredits each of the PME programs that provides JPME.[1] However, while the CJCS provides guidance to the military services regarding JPME and advice to the Secretary of Defense regarding PME, he does not run PME institutions, nor does he have authority to direct them, except for NDU. Other than NDU and the National Intelligence University, PME programs are run by service schools in the Air Force, Navy, Marine Corps, and Army. These programs operate using the resources they receive from the services, in the form of students and faculty offered by the service talent management practices and facilities and budgets provided to the institution by the services. These programs also operate under each service's educational policies and procedures, with oversight exercised by the host service and OSD. When exercising oversight, the host service and OSD consider the inputs received by the educational institutions, the service and joint operational needs and priorities, the priorities and policies articulated by the CJCS, and congressional requirements. These inputs are discussed further in the following sections.

CJCS Guidance and Oversight

In 2018, DoD's summary of the National Defense Strategy found that "PME has stagnated, focused more on the accomplishment of mandatory credit at the expense of lethality and ingenuity."[2] The May 2020 JPME vision statement by the JCS emphasizes the need to fully align PME and talent development, enabling the armed forces to better identify, develop, and utilize talent and to better serve DoD priorities by transitioning from a topic-based curriculum to an outcomes-based cur-

---

[1] Chairman of the Joint Chiefs of Staff Instruction 1800.01F, 2020, Section 8, "JPME Reviews and Evaluations," describing the Process of Accreditation for Joint Education (PAJE).

[2] Mattis, 2018, p. 8.

BOX 3.1

CJCS Priorities

CJCS priorities for the services' Talent Management functions

- Select the right talent for PME, hold students accountable for academic performance, utilize high-performing graduates in appropriate follow-on assignments, and reward continuous intellectual development.

- Focus on the learning continuum—training, experience, education, exercises, and self-improvement—and provide opportunities to refine and develop knowledge and skills outside PME.

- Provide appropriate incentives for selection, development, and management of PME faculty and instructors.

CJCS priorities for the PME programs run by the military educational institutions

- Effectively capture and assess student performance and potential.

- Include transregional and cross-domain training and experience, with jointness infused throughout PME and career development.

- Shift from topic-based to outcomes-based, responding to DoD objectives.

- Be innovative and continually assessed and adapted.

- Emphasize applied critical thinking skills and ingenuity, by incorporating active and experiential learning, including using gaming, exercises, and case studies grounded in history.

SOURCE: Adapted from Joint Chiefs of Staff, 2020.

riculum. To accomplish this, the vision outlines the following priorities for the services' Talent Management functions and PME institutions, as presented in Box 3.1.

Many of these priorities have been emphasized before. For example, the need for greater jointness and responsiveness to changing DoD demands in PME and career development was emphasized in the House Armed Services Committee's (HASC's) Skelton report in 1989.[3] PME has continued to be extensively studied and found in need of improvements.[4]

Concurrent with the JCS's new Vision publication, the CJCS's policy on PME, the OPMEP, was substantially revised in May 2020.[5] In prior versions, it established certain Joint Learning Areas (JLAs) that each intermediate and senior-level PME program's curriculum was required

---

[3] U.S. House of Representatives Committee on Armed Services, 1989.

[4] U.S. House of Representatives Committee on Armed Services, *Another Crossroads? Professional Military Education Two Decades After the Goldwater-Nichols Act and the Skelton Panel*, H.A.S.C. No. 111-67, May 20, 2009; Brenda S. Farrell, *Joint Military Education: Actions Needed to Implement DOD Recommendations for Enhancing Leadership Development*, U.S. Government Accountability Office, GAO-14029, October 2013; Brenda S. Farrell, *Professional Military Education: Programs Are Accredited, but Additional Information Is Needed to Assess Effectiveness*, U.S. Government Accountability Office, GAO-20-323, February 2020; Mayberry et al., 2021.

[5] Chairman of the Joint Chiefs of Staff Instruction 1800.01F, 2020.

to include, as well as certain education standards and practices. It also required that certain outcomes be considered in the assessment of each program, including Desired Leader Attributes (DLAs).[6] However, the revised policy now heavily emphasizes outcomes-based learning and requires each PME program to "[d]evelop and adopt an outcomes-based military education (OBME) approach in the development, delivery, and assessment of curricula."[7] It sets forth accreditation standards that measure both "the inputs [that] set the conditions for learning achievement and the outputs [that] provide the evidence of learning achievement."[8] It also now requires that each PME program use the JLAs and DLAs, as well as high-level CJCS guidance, "to develop mission-unique program learning outcomes."[9] It gives the Joint Staff, service chiefs, and combatant commanders increased responsibilities for oversight over the development and execution of OBME and program learning outcomes. Further details on OBME oversight, including accountabilities and milestones, are included in the recently released CJCS OBME manual.[10] The JLAs, Common Education Standards, desired PME outcomes, and DLAs are summarized in Box 3.2.

Aside from these rather fixed concepts, the CJCS also adopts a rotating set of special topics, called the Chairman's Special Areas of Emphasis. These topics can be changed every few years to help schools align their curricula with changing operational and strategic priorities, such as the return to great power competition, the importance of the information environment, and space as a warfighting domain.[11]

Military and Civilian Accreditation Complement Each Other

Perhaps the biggest challenge with CJCS oversight over PME is that, while the CJCS has oversight of PME, it lacks authority to direct changes to PME. In February 2020, prior to the CJCS's updated vision and OPMEP, the Government Accountability Office (GAO) studied the progress of PME.[12] It found several positive elements. For example, despite there being no CJCS or OSD requirement for civilian accreditation, all service intermediate and senior-level PME programs were accredited by their regional academic accrediting bodies, meaning that they possessed sufficiently rigorous academic quality to award master's degrees. In addition to civilian accreditation, the CJCS accredits every six years those

---

[6] Chairman of the Joint Chiefs of Staff Instruction 1800.01E, *Officer Professional Military Education Policy*, May 29, 2015 (superseded), enclosure E; Chairman of the Joint Chiefs of Staff Memorandum CM-0166-13, *Desired Leader Attributes for Joint Force 2020*, June 28, 2013.

[7] Chairman of the Joint Chiefs of Staff Instruction 1800.01F, 2020, p. 2.

[8] Chairman of the Joint Chiefs of Staff Instruction 1800.01F, 2020, p. A-C-1.

[9] Chairman of the Joint Chiefs of Staff Instruction 1800.01F, 2020, p. 3.

[10] Chairman of the Joint Chiefs of Staff Memorandum 1810.01E, *Outcomes-Based Military Education Procedures for Officer Professional Military Education*, April 1, 2022.

[11] See Joseph F. Dunford, Jr., "Special Areas of Emphasis for Joint Professional Military Education in Academic Years 2020 and 2021," memorandum for the chiefs of the military services and the President, National Defense University, CM-0108-19, May 6, 2019.

[12] Farrell, 2020.

BOX 3.2

Key Guidance for PME

JLAs

1. Strategic Thinking and Communication

2. The Profession of Arms

3. The Continuum of Competition, Conflict, and War

4. The Security Environment

5. Strategy and Joint Planning

6. Globally Integrated Operations

Common Education Standards (summarized)

1. Ensure joint acculturation, including an appropriate mix of joint faculty and students

2. Provide a rigorous and effective academic experience

3. Assess student achievement

4. Assess program through regular and rigorous review

5. Recruit and develop quality faculty and assess faculty performance

6. Provide appropriate institutional resources

PME Outcomes

1. Discern the military dimensions of a challenge affecting national interest; frame the issue at the policy level; and recommend viable military options within the overarching frameworks of globally integrated operations.

2. Anticipate and lead rapid adaptation and innovation during a dynamic period of acceleration in the rate of change in warfare under the conditions of great power competition and disruptive technology.

3. Conduct joint warfighting, at the operational to strategic levels, as all-domain, globally integrated warfare, including the ability to integrate allied and partner contributions.

4. Be a strategically minded warfighter or applied strategist who can execute and adapt strategy through campaigns and operations.

5. Demonstrate critical and creative thinking skills, interpersonal skills, and effective written, verbal, and visual communication skills to support the development and implementation of strategies and complex operations.

DLAs

1. Understand the security environment and contributions of all instruments of national power

2. Respond to surprise and uncertainty

3. Recognize change and lead transitions

4. Operate on intent through trust, empowerment, and understanding (mission command)

5. Make ethical decisions based on shared values of the profession of arms

6. Think critically and strategically in applying joint warfighting principles and concepts to joint operations.

SOURCE: Chairman of the Joint Chiefs of Staff Instruction 1800.01F, 2020, Enclosure A.

PME programs that award JPME credit, using the PAJE, in accordance with its OPMEP. At the time of the GAO report, the CJCS surveyed the PME programs' curricula to determine that they meet the appropriate JLAs and also assessed PME institutions' educational standards and practices. With respect to the JLAs in effect at the time, GAO found that the CJCS accredited all of the services' PME programs that award JPME, with the exception of the Marine Corps' intermediate program, which only partially met JLA requirements.[13]

Education Standards and Practices: An Ongoing Challenge

With respect to educational standards and practices required by the OPMEP, the results were less positive. In the most recent CJCS accreditation, all service intermediate and senior-level PME programs met or partially met all requirements, but only three of the eight programs met all requirements, and only two of the seven requirements were met by all programs. The common educational standards that were only partially met by at least one PME program related to developing joint awareness; employing active and highly effective instructional methods; assessing program effectiveness; providing institutional resources to support the educational process; and conducting quality faculty recruitment, selection, assignment, and performance assessment.[14] The standard related to faculty practices was the standard least likely to be fully met.[15] One of the significant findings was that the Navy consistently failed to send officers to the Army and Air Force PME programs, especially at the intermediate level, causing the programs to lack required joint representation. GAO found that no actions appeared to have been taken by OSD or the Navy to rectify this problem, and the Joint Staff officials lacked authority to direct the Navy to comply. As we discuss in Chapter 6, Navy representatives agreed that many leaders in the Navy would prefer to reserve a greater share of officers for operational assignments compared with the other services, rather than sending them to residential PME programs. Because JPME programs must maintain a mix of officers from all services, Navy desires conflict with the desires of the other services to send officers to these programs, because without enough Navy officers, the mix requirements cannot be met.

GAO found the oversight of PME to be problematic. It found that, while "OSD has had PME and JPME statutory oversight responsibilities for more than 30 years . . . , it is not well positioned to assess the effectiveness of the . . . programs, [because it] unofficially relinquished its responsibility for PME and JPME" to the CJCS.[16] The chairman, however, does not have authority to direct the programs (except for NDU) or to direct the services to comply with its policies. That function lies within OSD.

---

[13] Farrell, 2020, p. 17.

[14] Farrell, 2020, Table 5, p. 19.

[15] Farrell, 2020, Table 5, p. 19.

[16] Farrell, 2020, p. 26.

OSD Oversight

OSD acknowledged in a report to Congress in 2017 that it did not have a specific process for reviewing and overseeing PME.[17] However, OSD has begun to rectify this. In April 2022, DoD issued its first instruction on PME, *Military Education: Program Management and Administration* (DoDI 1322.35).[18] This new instruction complements the revised CJCS OPMEP and emphasizes the following:

- **Outcomes-based military education.** The instruction requires program-specific learning outcomes that focus on demonstrable performance in actual or simulated operational environments. Outcomes are labeled as *cognitive* (what students know), *affective* (what students value), and *psychomotor* (what students are able to do), and the outcomes require proficiency in strategic thinking, critical thinking, creative thinking, communicating, problem-framing, problem-solving, decisionmaking, and leadership. The instruction requires the service secretaries to monitor and periodically evaluate the outcome review processes, to validate the curriculum with external stakeholders, and to submit the program outcomes to OSD for certification to ensure that military education programs remain effective and current with evolving strategies and technologies, as indicated by OSD, Joint Staff, and military department priorities.

- **Student assessments.** The instruction requires schools to assess student outcomes in a manner that ascertains students' ability to perform successfully in operational environments. These assessments include direct assessments of students by the school, as well as indirect assessments, such as surveys of students, graduates, faculty, and supervisors at a graduate's follow-on unit to determine the degree to which the expectations for the role are met.

- **Talent Management.** The instruction directs the synchronization of military education policy with Talent Management. It requires that the services send to PME programs those officers with the greatest potential to contribute to mission success and for whom PME will be valuable to that success. It also requires the service secretaries to ensure that graduates of the programs receive challenging assignments equal to their newly acquired knowledge and skills. Individual PME academic performance is required to be a factor in deciding placement and promotion to greater responsibility and authority. It also requires that the services incentivize military members to serve as faculty at military education institutions, assess faculty member standards, and reward faculty with follow-on career opportunities equal to their performance.

---

[17] Office of the Under Secretary of Defense (Personnel & Readiness), *Department of Defense Report: A Review of Joint Professional Military Education Programs*, November 14, 2017, cited in Farrell, 2020, p. 26.

[18] DoDI 1322.35, 2022.

- **Selection criteria.** The instruction requires military education institutions to develop academic and professional selection standards that Talent Management can use to effectively screen students and faculty, to ensure that prospective students and faculty have the attributes and professional competencies to succeed.

- **Accountabilities.** The instruction requires the Assistant Secretary of Defense for Readiness and the Deputy Assistant Secretary of Defense for Force Education and Training to oversee military education and requires the service secretaries to conduct biennial military education program reviews. It also requires the development of metrics that enable valid comparisons of military education programs.
- **Civilian programs.** The instruction emphasizes the need to stimulate a wide variety of intellectual approaches to problem-solving and innovation by providing educational opportunities at multiple educational institutions, including civilian institutions.[19]

In June 2022, OSD reported the status of PME to HASC. It reported that PME institutions were surveying their alumni regarding how well the program prepared them for their subsequent assignments and found

---

[19] These bullets are adapted from the text of DoDI 1322.35, 2022.

that graduates reported being more adept as a result of PME.[20] PME institutions are also soliciting senior leader feedback on the degree to which PME graduates demonstrate proficiency in the program learning outcomes and on their skills and abilities.[21]

Service Oversight and Resourcing

Each service is responsible for the PME programs it runs, including the service military education institutions offering JPME credit. The service military education institutions operate under their individual policies and procedures responsive to the statutory, DoD, and CJCS requirements and guidance. They also operate within the institutional hierarchy of their service, including its Talent Management practices, which heavily influence both the education at the military education institutions and the utilization of that education.

The services fund their military education institutions with the appropriations they receive. This funding influences the quantity and quality of the civilian faculty and administrative staff that the military education institution can hire. The services also resource the military education institutions with an allotment of active-duty manpower for faculty to supplement the civilian faculty. The active-duty faculty is provisioned primarily from the host service, but in the case of JPME programs, each sister service is required to provide at least one faculty member as well (though this does not always happen). While each military education institution selects and hires its civilian faculty and staff, the service's Talent Management function selects and assigns the military education institution active-duty faculty. The military education institution may have conversations with the Talent Management function to influence the faculty it receives, but the decisionmaking rests with the service's Talent Management function. The incentives established by the Talent Management promotion and assignment practices appreciably influence the quality of the active-duty faculty.

Admissions

We summarize observations related to admissions in Table 3.1 by institutional type. Because observations for the civilian institutions were not different by type, we present a single entry for both types of civilian institutions, which are discussed later in this chapter.

Each technical military education institution admits students using its own selection standards based on a prospective student's academic preparation, like a civilian university. The service then decides whether to assign the admitted student to the military education institution. Strategic/operational programs, however, do not select students for admission. Instead, service Talent Management practices select which officers are sent to the military education institution as students. These selection decisions are made either centrally, through a selection board,

---

[20]   DoD, *HASC RFI on Professional Military Education*, June 15, 2022, p. 9.

[21]   DoD, 2022, pp. 9–10.

TABLE 3.1

Summary Observations on Admissions

	STRATEGIC/ OPERATIONAL	TECHNICAL
Military	• Decisions for admission to residential programs are based on service-convened boards that generally consider past operational expertise and future potential rather than academic aptitude • JPME-I programs offer distance learning without selection to maximize professional development participation • Educational institutions are not resourced to administer selection processes • Screening tests are not used to inform admission decisions	• Officers must be screened by institutions prior to selection by their service • Committee-based screening considers academic attainment in relevant technical areas and previously awarded technical degrees • Neither general nor technical screening tests are used to inform admission decisions
Civilian	• Committee decision is within academic department; no selection distinction is made between residential and hybrid offerings • Many programs admit significant numbers of international students who must pass English proficiency tests • Screening tests can be used but are now generally being phased out, and admission evaluations are moving toward consideration of the "whole person" construct	

or through the officer's career field. Decisions for residential strategic/ operational programs generally consider past operational expertise and future potential rather than academic aptitude. Screening tests are not used for program admissions. Efforts are made to maximize professional development participation for all officers via non-residential alternatives, especially at the JPME-I level. For both technical and strategic/ operational military education institution programs, service Talent Management functions also determine how graduates of the military education institution are utilized in follow-on assignments.

Essentially all the strategic/operational military institutions indicated that they did not have the staff capacity to screen candidates and perform an admissions function in addition to their educational mission, preferring to leave the task of selection and admission to the services.[22]

---

[22] The newly released DoDI 1322.35, 2022, para 4.2.f, requires military education institutions to "inform DoD Component talent management personnel about programs and develop personnel

One meaningful consequence of this approach is that the military educational institutions must work with whichever individuals the services send to them. As a result, as we learned from interviews, students are selected for PME not necessarily because they are best suited for an academic environment, but rather because they have been identified as future leaders regardless of academic credentials. The military education institutions also report that they have very little input into the international officers selected to attend by processes outside the school.

External Funding from Research Grants

To ensure that government entities carry out the intention of Congress in providing authorization and appropriations for their activities, such entities, including military education institutions, are not permitted to receive external funding without explicit statutory authority.[23] In order to receive funding from outside DoD, a military education institution must have a policy and authority allowing such. The military education institutions that provide technical education, such as AFIT and NPS, generally have such policies and authority and receive external funding from such sources as civilian universities, other government agencies, and private foundations. This external funding is usually provided for research. Strategic/operational military education institutions do not generally receive significant external funding from outside DoD and often do not have policies providing for the pursuit or receipt of such funding.

Comparison with Civilian Educational Institutions

The inputs into the military education system differ substantially from those found in civilian educational institutions offering similar education. Human and financial resourcing practices differ substantially, as does the institutions' ability to select students. Civilian institutions are able to recruit and select their own faculty, whereas military education institutions are only able to recruit and select their civilian faculty. While military education institutions are able to influence the military faculty assigned to them, the assignment decisions are ultimately made by the services' Talent Management practices. This faculty selection process can vary considerably by service, as some services may require that officers formally apply and have to be interviewed, while others implement less formalized processes relative to specifying prerequisite teaching acumen and experiences. Civilian institutions are also able to apply their own admission standards and select their own students, often using a whole-person evaluation considering past education and professional experiences, a statement of purpose, recommendations, and an interview. Strategic/operational military education institutions, on the other hand, receive students selected by the services' Talent Management practices (which are a de facto whole-person approach

---

screening mechanisms to ensure prospective students have the attributes and professional competencies to contribute to peer learning and to succeed in the program."

23   See, generally, the Antideficiency Act (31 U.S.C. 1341–1342).

based on past professional military experiences and judgments of the officer's future potential) and do not select their own students.

Financial resourcing practices also differ between civilian schools and military education institutions, which causes the incentives involved in civilian education to differ from military education institutions. Civilian educational institutions receive their funding from donors, grants, and students. If civilian institutions do not respond to the needs of their students, by adapting their faculty hiring and curriculum development accordingly, market forces will likely cause the students to go elsewhere. Military education institutions, by contrast, are not faced with the same market forces. They receive their funding in annual allotments, and their students are assigned by annual quotas.

The involvement of international students offers military education institutions a needed and broad diversity of concepts, experiences, and perspectives. The value of incorporating such students is a long-term investment in developing key relationships, inculcating American values and doctrine, and instilling a shared sense of security cooperation. However, there is also a counterargument for allowing considerable numbers of international students: the impact of limited English proficiency, the requirement to teach to a lower level of overall expertise, and a limit to sharable information due to classification. Like the military education institutions, many of the civilian schools studied offer a mix of in-residence and remote education options. Most of the civilian schools compete for global talent and enroll a significant number of international students. These international students are overwhelmingly concentrated in in-residence programs and often constitute a significant funding source for the civilian programs.

CHAPTER 4

Processes in PME: Teaching, Research, Engagement, and Service

The second core component of PME and its institutions is the set of processes involved in the actual work of education: curriculum, faculty hiring and practices, graduation requirements, and the like. By better understanding these processes, one will be able to see distinctions between military educational institutions, compare military educational approaches with those of peer civilian institutions, and more clearly perceive the structures that drive educational delivery for service members and select civilians.

Curriculum and Teaching Methods

We summarize observations related to curriculum in Table 4.1 by institutional type. We discuss these observations in more detail after the table.

Within military education institutions, a variety of curricula have been established to meet the needs of the services. These are described in the following section.

TECHNICAL INSTITUTIONS FOCUS PRIMARILY ON RELATED LEARNING, AS WELL AS RESEARCH

For the technically focused military institutions, such as AGS or AFIT, courses focus on math, engineering, and formal and natural sciences. They offer research opportunities for students based in these areas. Discussions with leaders of these institutions revealed that developing technical expertise and contributing to research were two clear priorities.

TABLE 4.1

Summary Observations on Curriculum and Teaching Methods

	STRATEGIC/OPERATIONAL	TECHNICAL
Military	• Broad curriculum focused on leadership and military strategy • Diverse, small seminar teams, case studies, guest speakers, practicums, job-relevant projects • In-residence, online, and hybrid offerings • Classified information required for some topics	• Curriculum focused on theoretical and scientific basis of military-related applications while also conducting practical real-world work and research • Combination of small technical classrooms and laboratory experiences with some seminar opportunities • Classified information used for science and engineering topics
Civilian	• Broad curriculum focused on such disciplines as public administration, international relations, or management • Individual and small-group work, guest speakers, case studies for more-qualitative offerings, some gaming, practicums focused on real problems • In-residence (sometimes allowing either day or evening study) and online offerings	• Curriculum focused on understanding theoretical and scientific basis of general technical applications while also conducting practical real-world work and research • Combination of small technical classrooms and laboratory experiences • In-residence and online offerings

STRATEGICALLY AND OPERATIONALLY FOCUSED MILITARY EDUCATION INSTITUTIONS CONCENTRATE ON CORE LEADERSHIP SKILLS, POLICY, AND STRATEGY

Institutions that focus on broader issues of strategy, regional- or subject-specific topics, and policy, such as NDU and USAWC, offer courses that focus more on aspects of policy, strategy, leadership, and implementation, rather than on the technical or scientific issues addressed by other military institutions.

Interviews and responses provided by strategic/operational-focused military education institutions suggested that courses are constructed across several common themes. These are critical thinking, effective decisionmaking, leadership, and an emphasis on regional- and issue-specific focus. Many students who graduate from these institutions have already been placed in leadership positions and will likely end up in positions of even greater authority upon graduation. Therefore, honing general skills around areas of policy, implementation, and decisionmaking aligns with likely future needs from officers, as opposed to the more technical kinds of subject areas that are addressed in the academic programs at AFIT, NPS, and AGS.

Especially for strategic/operational-focused military institutions, graduates are frequently exposed to course material that covers current and emerging subject areas of importance to the national defense. There was recognition that some subject areas (such as counterterrorism), while not unimportant, had been overtaken in relevance to the current strategic needs and objectives of the U.S. military, such as great power competition. It was not surprising, then, that throughout the interviews conducted, institutional leaders emphasized that they were keen to adopt new courses that addressed the most-pressing challenges faced by the nation (for example, introducing course material to address Indo-Pacific issues, as opposed to continuing an emphasis on counterterrorism operations). In many cases, they were able to do so, given the structure of hiring that allows for greater flexibility to bring on new faculty with relevant expertise.

IN COURSE DELIVERY, SEMINARS ARE KEY

An essential element of course delivery, as noted by most school administrators interviewed, is the collection of seminars in which each student participates while enrolled, particularly in strategic/operational-focused military institutions. These seminars cover a range of militarily relevant subjects, and while they enhance intellectual growth in important strategic and policy domains, they also serve the purpose of providing stronger networks between peers and future colleagues, whether within the same service, across different services, or even throughout the interagency. The seminars particularly enhance relationships and network formation because of the way in which they facilitate conversation among students, which was viewed by administrators as a strong benefit for students in terms of both academic experience and professional development.

CASE STUDIES ARE USED MORE IN STRATEGIC/ OPERATIONAL INSTITUTIONS THAN IN TECHNICAL INSTITUTIONS

One important aspect of this discussion of curriculum and course delivery is the use of case studies. Academic literature notes that case studies are most often successfully employed when addressing such issues as critical and situational thinking, decisionmaking, and understanding effective processes; they are typically less effective, according to this literature, in areas of transmitting hard skills, as well as more technical, factual information (e.g., mathematics for accounting).[1] Across our study of military educational institutions, essentially all of them reported that they utilize case studies to conduct teaching in one way or another, pri-

---

[1] Margaret Healy and Maeve McCutcheon, "Teaching with Case Studies: An Empirical Investigation of Accounting Lecturers' Experiences," *Accounting Education*, Vol. 19, No. 6, 2010; Jenice P. Stewart and Thomas W. Dougherty, "Using Case Studies in Teaching Accounting: A Quasi-Experimental Study," *Accounting Education*, Vol. 2, No. 1, 1993; P. K. Raju and Chetan S. Sankar, "Teaching Real-World Issues Through Case Studies," *Journal of Engineering Education*, Vol. 88, No. 4, 1999; Mehdi Farashahi and Mahdi Tajeddin, "Effectiveness of Teaching Methods in Business Education: A Comparison Study on the Learning Outcomes of Lectures, Case Studies and Simulations," *International Journal of Management Education*, Vol. 16, No. 1, 2018.

marily to improve critical thinking skills. They use case studies for these purposes rather than to transmit specific facts and technical knowledge, which they see as better suited for delivery through traditional lectures and relevant experiential labs.

The technical military educational institutions (particularly NPS, AFIT, and AGS) report that they rely less on case studies than the strategic/operational institutions do. Given the extent to which the technical institutions are seeking to impart a specific kind of factual knowledge not as easily learned from a historical case study, this is not surprising, though some lessons regarding innovation and best practices for research can be learned from case studies. As a result, the kinds of case studies used by the technical institutions focus less on issues of strategy and more on issues of how research has been effectively conducted and what can position research teams to be most successful.

The strategic/operational military institutions report a broader application of case studies, including lessons learned from previous conflicts and military campaigns, strategy development processes, policy implementation issues, and subject- or region-specific topics. These kinds of case studies are utilized to facilitate group discussion and critical thinking development. Throughout the interviews conducted and responses acquired, case studies were clearly identified as a helpful teaching tool and were understood to be an especially effective means for imparting strategic and decisionmaking knowledge.

The institutions did not report any specific challenges associated with utilizing case studies or barriers to their use other than the continued development and updating of relevant case study materials. For military institutions, decisions regarding the use of case studies primarily involve the question of what academic contexts are most appropriate for specific kinds of case studies. Overall, the way in which case studies are utilized by military educational institutions aligns closely with best practices for their use as characterized by the academic literature. As noted, scholarship indicates that case studies are often less helpful for learning hard technical skills (such as advanced mathematics) but that they are particularly useful when it comes to improving decisionmaking ability, strategic thinking, and historical understanding to navigate present-day contexts more effectively.

While there are some noticeable differences between military and civilian academic institutions, they are very much in sync when it comes to how case studies are utilized in the classroom. Like military institutions, civilian schools report that they primarily utilize case studies for conducting group work, enhancing critical and situational thinking, and reviewing decisionmaking processes. Other aspects of programs, especially those that are more technical or focused on transmitting sets of scientific or quantitative facts, see far less use of case studies in civilian institutions. In this way, the practices of civilian academic institutions around the use of case studies closely reflect best practices as defined by the literature, and they also dovetail with the way in which case studies are generally employed in military academic institutions.

> While there are some noticeable differences between military and civilian academic institutions, they are very much in sync when it comes to how case studies are utilized in the classroom.

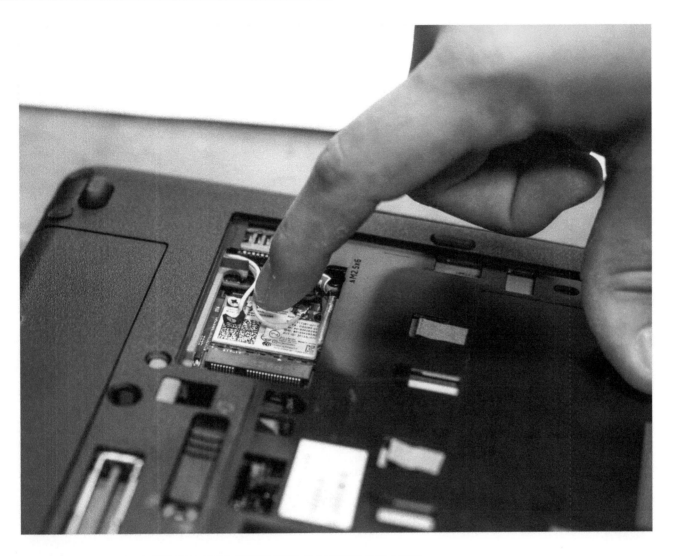

MILITARY EDUCATION SOMETIMES REQUIRES USE OF CLASSIFIED INFORMATION

A notable difference between civilian and military educational institutions—and not limited to the use of case studies, but across the entirety of the curriculum—is the use of classified information in military educational settings. There is simply no comparable aspect of civilian education that involves discussions, technical instruction, or case studies centered on classified material. The military educational institutions have both the facilities and the operational need to utilize classified information for the education of their students, most of whom will go on to perform responsibilities in a classified setting. This is an important distinguishing factor for military educational institutions, and one that is highly unlikely to be replicated in civilian educational institutions. The military educational institutions, therefore, serve a critical purpose in educating officers using the best available—and sometimes classified—information to prepare them to either deter or fight and win wars with the nation's adversaries.

Demands for classified education continue to evolve based on updates to joint operational concepts. Our discussions with the Joint

TABLE 4.2

Summary Observations on Faculty Management Practices

	STRATEGIC/ OPERATIONAL	TECHNICAL
Military	• Mix of full-time civilians, military officers, and adjuncts (term appointments) across multiple disciplines • Institutions select civilian faculty • Services are largely responsible for selecting officers as faculty, although institutions may provide input • Civilian faculty are appointed to fixed terms, which may be renewed based on performance in teaching, research, and service • Military faculty bring recent knowledge of the operational and strategic context • Adjunct faculty provide short-term, focused expertise	• Considerable variance in faculty mix across technical programs • Most institutions have military officers but fewer than in strategic/operational institutions • Institutions select civilian faculty • Services are largely responsible for selecting officers as faculty, although institutions may provide input • Some offer tenure to civilians, which is granted by a committee evaluation of teaching, research, and service • If employed, military faculty bring recent knowledge of the operational and strategic context • Adjunct faculty bring field-specific expertise, often essential to the program
Civilian	• Mix of full-time faculty and adjuncts • Full-time faculty often on tenure track, but professors of practice may be appointed for renewable terms • Sometimes extensive use of adjuncts to lower costs and add professional expertise compared with the tenure-track faculty	

Staff highlight their concerns that JPME programs, especially war colleges, are not sufficiently aligned with changing warfighting demands. The Joint Staff specifically call for increasing these institutions' capacity to provide education using classified materials and to conduct classified wargames. Such increases will likely require expanded classified facilities and additional faculty with necessary clearances.

Faculty Management Practices

We summarize observations related to faculty management practices in Table 4.2 by institutional type. We discuss these observations in more detail after the table.

Central to PME is the question of who is teaching students. For almost every institution we interviewed, there was a noticeable difference between military educational institutions and civilian schools around the question of personnel and hiring.

MILITARY FACULTY ARE MANAGED BY THE SERVICES

To begin, military institutions employ officers as instructors, whereas civilian institutions have few, if any, individuals connected to the military teaching in their classrooms. Military faculty are selected directly by each service through the services' respective assignment processes (in which officers might express a preference to be assigned as faculty). While staffing their own schools, the services also bear a responsibility to provide faculty for sister service and joint institutions. However, these obligations are not always fulfilled; multiple institutions described difficulty in consistently filling sister service faculty positions in their own service's schools.

Across the military educational institutions, it is common practice for military faculty to stay for two to four years before a new rotation of faculty is brought in. This practice aids in maintaining curricular currency, as new faculty with relevant experiences and expertise can teach on subjects of importance to the existing priorities of the service. Many military educational institutions frequently update their curricula, which means that there is a regular need for relevant experience, which can be provided in this rotational system.

In terms of the kinds of individuals brought in as military faculty, two types most commonly emerged from discussions with military educational institutions. The first consists of selected recent graduates of the school, who are sometimes kept on as instructors following the completion of their studies. The second type, which is more prevalent than the first, consists of officers who are nearing retirement. For many institutions interviewed, an assignment as a military faculty member was often viewed as a step off the path of promotion to higher-level assignments (such as general or flag officer). These individuals, in many cases, serve a three- or four-year rotation and then retire.

While some individuals do continue on to higher ranks after a faculty stint, it appears most common for a military educational institution teaching post to be the last stop for an officer before retirement. This reality reflects an attitudinal shift among the services in the value of teaching for career development and advancement. As one institution noted, in the mid-20th century, promotion to the highest levels almost always required faculty experience. The fact that a faculty position might be viewed as a liability regarding promotion or even as an officer's final post is indicative of the change in how the armed forces value teaching as it relates to career advancement.

One aspect of career advancement that is viewed as important is joint credit, which is a requirement to be considered for promotion to general or flag officer.[2] Currently, military faculty members receive joint credit when they teach at a joint or sister service senior institution but do not receive it at their own service institutions. Therefore, an officer who wishes to remain eligible for promotion beyond O-6 and is selected for a faculty assignment at their own service institution must also com-

---

[2] DoDI 1300.19, *DoD Joint Officer Management (JOM) Program*, Office of the Under Secretary of Defense for Personnel and Readiness, April 3, 2018.

plete a joint qualifying tour in another assignment. Having to complete two assignments outside the core operational functions of their service leads to a disincentive for individuals to pursue faculty opportunities.

One other area where there is less uniformity is in the realm of the military/civilian faculty balance. While perhaps not surprising, several of the technical institutions tend to rely more on civilian faculty compared with strategic/operational ones. While a balance of faculty may be heavily skewed in favor of military faculty at many strategic/operational military institutions, schools like NPS and AGS are more heavily weighted toward civilian faculty (with AFIT sitting closer to a 50/50 split). In fact, AGS is entirely composed of adjunct civilian faculty.

"TENURE WITHOUT TENURE" IS THE NORM FOR CIVILIAN FACULTY IN MILITARY EDUCATIONAL INSTITUTIONS

While they are not subject to the same selection and rotation processes as military faculty, civilian faculty have a well-defined relationship with military educational institutions with respect to hiring and retention practices.

Most civilian institutions operate with a traditional tenure model, with some space for pure teaching roles among adjunct faculty. For example, multiple civilian schools hire adjunct faculty solely for teaching, whereas tenure-track faculty are also hired and then expected to split time between teaching and research. Military institutions do not employ a traditional tenure model, however. Rather, they primarily utilize what was frequently characterized as a "tenure without tenure" model. Under this form of management, instructors at military educational institutions are often hired for periods of up to five years at a time, with the possibility of the hiring recurring every (up to) five years. As indicated in conversations with military educational institutions, a recurring appointment is the standard outcome, so long as an individual instructor continues to perform well in the classroom and produce an appropriate amount of research.

The military schools emphasized that this model, as opposed to a traditional tenure model, brings several benefits. To begin, it ensures that the schools maintain the ability to control quality of instruction. But more importantly, it allows for greater flexibility in introducing new courses and curricula if a pressing subject issue needs to be taught in the institution. In other words, by being able to bring on and/or rotate out different faculty with different kinds of subject expertise, the institutions are better able to adapt to a changing strategic landscape and ensure that students are receiving the kind of education they need to make sense of the most relevant strategic, military, and policy concepts that the armed forces must navigate.

The "tenure without tenure" model was viewed by the institutions as an effective means for maintaining quality, flexibility, and adaptability in today's complex strategic environment. This kind of policy is obviously different from the traditional tenure model of many civilian institutions, perhaps raising the question of whether faculty at military institutions have full academic freedom in the way that counterparts with tenure at civilian institutions might be considered to have. However, the military institutions emphasized in interviews that they protect the academic freedom of their faculty and that the standards of a "tenure without tenure" model still allow for robust research and freedom of inquiry among their faculty.

USE OF ADJUNCT AND VISITING FACULTY VARIES WIDELY

The number of adjunct faculty can vary significantly by institution. Some schools use a minimal number of adjunct faculty, preferring to emphasize full-time positions that are tightly connected to the institution. Others, such as the AGS, are essentially entirely composed of adjunct faculty, who lend their expertise depending on the kind of research and instruction that needs to be completed.

Some of the strategic/operational military institutions also maintain long-standing arrangements with civilian federal agencies (such as the Department of State and the Department of Homeland Security) to detail staff as visiting faculty, enriching the institutions' coverage of current topics that intersect military and civilian authorities.

Graduation Requirements and Academic Support

We summarize observations related to graduation requirements and academic support in Table 4.3 by institutional type. We discuss these observations in more detail after the table.

While some important differences exist between the types of military educational institutions, most follow a standard set of procedures for moving students through an academic program. For instance, with some moderate variation, the military educational institutions require students to successfully complete a series of mandatory courses with a satisfactory grade, coupled with either a final set of written or oral exams or an independent research project. For programs focused on advanced technical research (especially those granting doctoral degrees), the independent research process is more intensive. Nevertheless, the process of coursework combined with exams or a research project is nearly universal in the realm of military educational institutions. In many ways, this is like the instructional organization of civilian universities, which also emphasize coursework, exams, and independent research. One noticeable difference is that civilian institutions, in addition to a set number of courses, exams, and research requirements, often strive to give their students experiential learning opportunities through such programs as internships with local organizations focused on their area of study. For example, one large civilian institution explicitly works to connect students with internship opportunities so that they can gain an applied understanding of what they are learning in the classroom. Though not always required, these experiential learning opportunities represent a break with the typical mode of delivery for military educational institutions. In part, this is because military

The process of coursework combined with exams or a research project is nearly universal in the realm of military educational institutions.

TABLE 4.3

Summary Observations on Graduation Requirements and Academic Support

	STRATEGIC/OPERATIONAL	TECHNICAL
Military	• Graduation requires completing specified curriculum, typically with 3.0 (out of 4.0) grade point average (GPA) or better	• Graduation requires completing a specified curriculum, typically with 3.0 (out of 4.0) GPA or better
	• Some institutions offer academic support based on early assessments	• Most academic issues are avoided by the admissions review of student preparation
	• Some institutions offer support centers, such as in writing	• All institutions expect faculty to support students when they observe challenges
	• All institutions expect faculty to support students when they observe challenges	• With admissions reviews and faculty support, essentially all students graduate except for a few with behavioral issues (e.g., plagiarism, overall misconduct) or unrelated family matters
	• With academic support provided, essentially all students graduate in residential programs except for a few with behavioral issues (e.g., plagiarism, overall misconduct) or unrelated family matters	
	• Lower graduation rates for online options are due to self-withdrawal	
Civilian	• Graduation requires completing specified curriculum, typically with 3.0 (out of 4.0) GPA or better	
	• Academic adviser assigned to each student to monitor progress	
	• Tutoring and mentoring are offered through broader university services, online tutoring is offered for individuals weak in either English or math, and leave of absence can be granted for personal matters	
	• Because of rigorous admission process and faculty academic support, essentially all students graduate except for a few with behavioral issues (e.g., plagiarism, overall misconduct) or unrelated family matters	

students are already a part of the organization in which they will serve upon graduation and have significant applied experience before beginning their educational programs.

Military educational institutions do report that they face situations in which students are not performing at a satisfactory level. Here, there is some differentiation between military institutions. While some, such as the technical institutions, will not allow a student to continue to pursue the highest achievable degree if a C grade or lower is earned in any one course, others, including the strategic/operational institutions, opt for the provision of academic support and even remediation for students who do not meet standards on their first attempt. Many strategic/operational institutions have academic and writing centers designed specifically for the task of assisting students who need more intensive help with academic tasks so that officers can continue through the program and earn the necessary degree, certificate, or credit. In some cases, students are allowed to retake a course to earn a requisite grade.

The strategic/operational institution approach is, therefore, more like traditional civilian master's programs, which also seek out ways for students to meet required standards rather than shutting the door to a degree opportunity if a course is not passed satisfactorily on a first attempt. Because both military and civilian institutions have incentives for ensuring that each student passes the course of study, their approaches to corrective academic action ultimately look similar. In both cases, some students do drop out of the course of study; however, this is very rarely the case because of academic performance issues. Oftentimes, withdrawal from a military academic program is a result of other personal or professional issues and/or responsibilities that arise, making continuation of the program untenable for the individual in question. This does mean that, in practice, failure to complete a military academic program is rarely a function of inability to meet graduation requirements. In interviews, the military institutions noted that this reality is largely a credit to the academic support provided to students throughout their time in the educational environment, rather than a lack of standards enforcement. The question of how these graduation requirements are then connected to roles in future services is an important one and will be addressed later in the report.

Educational Delivery Methods

In the past decade, military educational institutions have operated in both a remote and an in-person capacity, but the trend toward remote opportunities has accelerated in the coronavirus pandemic era, with health concerns forcing institutions to suddenly move away from in-person instruction during the pandemic. However, the majority of PME and other military educational institutions have some need for in-person learning, whether it is a function of laboratory work, lessons that require secured facilities, or seminars that simply benefit in significant ways from in-person meetings. This means that more certificates can be offered via online methods, while more research- and discussion-based degree programs are offered in person.

Conversations with institutional leaders revealed that the move toward increased remote offerings has come with both benefits and drawbacks. For instance, remote options for teaching represent a significant asset insofar as more individuals can now take advantage of educational opportunities. If officers or enlisted personnel are required to perform duties in locations other than an educational institution's main campus, the remote option allows for participation where it may not have been a possibility in the past. For those who otherwise could not have access to additional military education, this is a noteworthy benefit. However, trade-offs are always involved, as the nature and quality of teaching and discussion may suffer because of not having in-person engagement with professors and peers. In conversations with institutional leaders, it was clear that the intangibles of in-person discussions during seminars made that aspect of academic engagement highly valuable.

Moreover, in addition to missing out on some of the relational and educational benefits of in-person instruction and discussion, officers and enlisted personnel who take remote courses while serving in a full-time position do not enjoy the same degree of time and space provided for reprieve from military duties to more fully engage with the academic material over a period of time. For students who attend military academic programs in person, there is significant time and space allocated for the pursuit of intellectual life without the burden of military duties; this kind of break from the intense physical and mental strain of ordinary military life likely confers a significant benefit on those individuals who attend academic programs in person, given the increased opportunity for intellectual engagement and refreshment.

Taking into consideration these trade-offs between remote and in-person learning, the DoD educational enterprise—much like its civilian counterparts—is working to understand what the best combination of remote and in-person learning is for optimizing student outcomes. For civilian institutions, similarly to discussions with military educational leaders, a premium was placed on in-person instruction, while administrators also noted that more-flexible remote and part-time offerings allowed an additional range of students to take advantage of available programs. While civilian institutions generally saw relatively more international students participate in in-person instruction and relatively more domestic students participate in remote instruction, the same set of trade-offs between flexibility/opportunity and instructional value appeared to apply.

Accreditation

As described in Chapter 3, the Joint Staff review all JPME-granting institutions using the PAJE. The PAJE is a body appointed by the J-7 that both focuses on "joint education and provides oversight, assessment, and improvement" and ensures that professional learning outcomes are "relevant and measurable."[3] The PAJE is therefore also closely linked to the process of oversight when it comes to transitions of military educational institutions to OBME. As defined in military guidance,[4] the PAJE is "generally guided by accepted civilian accreditation standards." Through this process, accreditation is granted for six years, to be reviewed and renewed every six years from the initial date of accreditation.[5]

In addition to undergoing this process, the military educational institutions in this study have met civilian accreditation requirements from the relevant regional accrediting bodies. For example, NDU is accredited by the Middle States Commission on Higher Education. The most recently accredited institution is the AGS. There are several benefits that flow from civilian accreditation, the first of which is the

---

[3] Mayberry et al., 2021, p. 47.

[4] Joint Chiefs of Staff, "Officer Professional Military Education Policy (OPMEP)," Chairman of the Joint Chiefs of Staff Instruction 1800:01D, July 15, 2009; Ch. 1, December 15, 2011; Directive Current as of September 5, 2012, p. F-1.

[5] Joint Chiefs of Staff, 2012.

authority to grant master's and doctoral degrees. This is critical for the credibility of the education offered by military educational institutions. There are benefits to being accredited besides degree-granting authority, however. In the eyes of the public, an accredited institution is likelier to have a significantly enhanced reputation relative to institutions that are not accredited. Civilian accreditation is an asset for military educational institutions particularly in efforts to hire faculty, who are certainly cognizant of whether the school they would join is or is not accredited. There are important implications for hiring, then, that come with becoming and staying accredited by meeting civilian academic standards. This will be an important aspect of the military's efforts to best educate its officers and enlisted personnel, particularly given that the quality of faculty is in no small part influenced by accreditation status.

In this respect, civilian institutions highly resemble their military counterparts, insofar as accreditation is essential for public reputation and hiring, with the additional imperative of student recruitment. Civilian institutions must maintain accreditation to grant their degrees, an authority without which they would hardly be able to recruit students to attend. In fact, accreditation is likely of even greater importance to civilian institutions than to strategic/operational military institutions, which have a second process (PAJE) for ensuring that their students are achieving desired learning outcomes.

Research, Engagement, and Service

We summarize observations related to research, engagement, and service in Table 4.4 by institutional type.

In discussions with institutional leaders, research was consistently raised as a central line of effort within the PME enterprise. Whether at a highly technical level in Ph.D.-granting programs or at a more strategic/

TABLE 4.4

Summary Observations on Research, Engagement, and Service

	STRATEGIC/ OPERATIONAL	TECHNICAL
Military	• Research is viewed as complementary to the educational mission, as well as providing broadening opportunities to students	• Research is viewed as complementary to the educational mission, as well as providing broadening opportunities to students
	• There is often a strong linkage between faculty research and teaching responsibilities	• There is usually a strong linkage between faculty research and teaching responsibilities
Civilian	• Tenure-track faculty typically are expected to produce significant academic research, which may be only loosely related to their teaching responsibilities	
	• External funding can be an important source of research support	

operational and theoretical level in PME programs, both students and faculty are regularly encouraged, and in many cases required, to pursue their own research. One theme that clearly emerged from these discussions was that there was, for faculty, a symbiotic relationship between teaching and research. While it may be easy to assume that any time devoted to research is time that detracts from teaching efforts, administrators were clear that the independent work conducted by faculty enhances their ability to bring relevant and robust lessons to the classroom. Of course, for many institutions that operate with a "tenure without tenure" system, conducting research is a prerequisite for continued employment, which makes for multiple incentives to pursue independent research. Not only does independent research often bolster the quality of classroom instruction—it also serves as an incentive to earn reappointment as a faculty member. To maintain good standing, faculty must teach effectively and make relevant contributions to knowledge. Faculty are thus given time to conduct research, and it is usually independently directed; in other words, the military institutions themselves are not able to dictate to faculty what kind of research they should conduct. For institutions that are seeking to address specific, military-relevant issues, this can be a source of friction, as schools might desire a greater voice in determining the subjects of faculty research. While faculty are provided with resources internally for their research, there is minimal external funding in most institutions.

This model of research within military educational institutions largely resembles civilian counterparts, where full-time faculty are expected to regularly conduct independent research. This is similar in that the research is self-directed and in that research is an expectation for full-time faculty (adjunct faculty are more commonly brought in only to teach courses, rather than to also conduct research). One point of difference is that civilian universities often allow full-time faculty to apply for research grants, making external funding a resource for faculty at civilian institutions that generally does not exist at military educational institutions.

Aside from research, military education institutions also engage in outreach and service activities to deepen their connections with the services, the joint community, other U.S. government agencies, and international partners. A study conducted at the same time as this one found that military education institutions provide their faculty as guest speakers and consultants and convene meetings and conferences to build connections across the communities they serve.[6]

Following the discussion of processes in this chapter, we next turn to the outcomes of PME.

---

[6] See Quentin E. Hodgson, Charles A. Goldman, Jim Mignano, and Karishma R. Mehta, *Educating for Evolving Operational Domains: Cyber and Information Education in the Department of Defense and the Role of the College of Information and Cyberspace*, RAND Corporation, RR-A1548-1, 2022. While that study focused on the domains of cyberspace and the information environment, we think that these conclusions are broadly applicable across domains. Our study did not examine engagement and service specifically.

CHAPTER 5

Outcomes: Qualified Officers and Institutions

A s discussed in Chapter 3, the JCS vision for PME has been articulated in such a way that effective utilization in follow-on assignments is now a key priority for the military educational enterprise. This prioritization is necessarily predicated both on appropriate selection of military talent for PME and on the upholding of high standards for academic performance, such that the institutions themselves are not merely a box to check, but a military resource for ingenuity and lethality. An important question thus becomes how well PME institutions are bringing their efforts into alignment with the JCS vision, which will be examined in this chapter by more closely looking at how outputs are understood and measured within military educational institutions.

We summarize observations related to outcomes in Table 5.1 by institutional type. We discuss these observations in more detail after the table.

Evaluations of Graduate Performance

Since roughly 2016, military educational institutions have been moving to an outcomes-based approach to teaching and academic performance. This means that defined and measurable indicators must be set in place for students. It also means that the schools all have some form of evaluations for the attending officers and enlisted personnel. For example, most schools identify distinguished graduates within their respective programs. This group is frequently limited to the top 10 percent of graduates.

Schools have done much work in developing ways to evaluate student performance throughout and at the conclusion of students' academic experiences. However, it is not clear that these evaluations are used in a meaningful capacity by services to inform future assignments in the graduates' careers. For example, while the schools generally do identify distinguished graduates, the connection between academic performance and future assignments is tenuous at best. Of the more technical schools (AGS, AFIT, and NPS), follow-on assignments upon completion of an advanced degree are often connected to the specific

TABLE 5.1

Summary Observations on Outcomes

	STRATEGIC/OPERATIONAL	TECHNICAL
Military	• A closed system in which the students continue in their careers after graduation	• A closed system in which the students continue in their careers after graduation
	• Loose connection between educational attainment and subsequent assignments	• Closer connection between educational attainment and subsequent assignments
	• Limited feedback from subsequent performance to schools	• Some feedback from subsequent performance to schools
Civilian	• An open system with loose links between schools and employers	
	• Limited feedback from subsequent performance to schools	
	• Sometimes general information on graduate earnings or employer satisfaction is available in surveys and rankings	

disciplines studied while at the institution, but they are not necessarily connected to academic performance while at the institution. In other words, graduating with distinction is no guarantee of a specific kind of placement following the educational experience. For the JPME institutions, there is often even less connection between evaluation and follow-on assignments. Throughout the interviews conducted with the academic institutions, as will be detailed more closely in the following section, the actual process of student evaluations was largely viewed as being disconnected from future assignments, with the schools themselves being unclear on how the services made decisions about which students were placed in which roles upon graduation. One exception to this general rule was MCU, where the school director has a specific say in where marines are assigned after graduation. Other than MCU, though, there was an apparent disconnect between the schools' role in evaluating students and the services' decisions about future career positions for students.

According to our interviews, the services and the schools do not directly track the utilization of skills and knowledge learned at PME institutions. As a result, we did not find any clear evidence on how well graduates are utilized and whether the skills they may learn in PME are used in their subsequent assignments.

If the JCS vision of outcomes-based education is to be realized, the services and educational institutions will require systematic information on how well graduates perform in their subsequent assignments. Better tools will be required to measure graduate performance and feed that information back to schools so that they can adjust their curricula and teaching methods to meet service needs.[1]

Similarities and Differences Between Civilian and Military Academic Institutions

When it comes to student evaluations and utilization, civilian and military institutions are like one another. This is especially the case insofar as there is little tracking of effective placement in postgraduate work positions (i.e., placement into positions that make use of the degree or academic credit earned). According to interviews conducted with five civilian institutions, while career services are frequently offered to students, the schools themselves play a minimal role in placement and, beyond maintaining alumni networks, do very little to measure whether their students are utilizing the degree-specific skills acquired in their programs in their subsequent job placements. Some graduate program rankings and institution-specific surveys do collect information on graduate earnings or general employer satisfaction with programs.

Similarly, military academic institutions have thorough evaluation processes in place for students while they are attending school but next to no involvement in the selection of future career posts or follow-on evaluation of the extent to which the academic experience prepared the individuals in question for their next assignments.

On its face, the absence of any kind of measurement surrounding effective utilization makes more sense for civilian institutions, as they are not also the future employers of their students. Once a student graduates from, say, Purdue University, the institution no longer has a direct connection to the student's life and work. And as long as students in civilian schools obtain jobs after graduation, that statistic is usually enough for civilian institutions to determine that they are preparing students for future employment. For the military, however, the circumstances are naturally much different, as officers in PME programs do not leave the military upon graduation but rather step into their next role for the armed forces. Because the military is investing in its own people through PME, it would make sense for there to be a more concentrated effort to appropriately place and utilize graduates—or at least to measure the extent to which skills learned in PME and technical education programs are being utilized in follow-on assignments. One might think that this would be a natural step to take given the recent emphasis in military schooling on outcomes-based education. However, for both the schools and the services, this step does not appear to happen.

Supporting the JCS Vision for Force Development

As noted in Chapter 3, increased alignment between PME and professional development is a significant priority for the JCS. This includes identifying the right talent for PME, ensuring that selected individu-

> Because the military is investing in its own people through PME, it would make sense for there to be a more concentrated effort to appropriately place and utilize graduates.

---

[1] This topic is discussed extensively in Mayberry et al., 2021, which reviews a subset of the institutions covered in this study.

als are learning meaningful skills rather than passing through a box-checking exercise, and then effectively utilizing those newly learned skills. A clear opportunity for alignment thus runs through these three steps, but, as conversations with various institutions have highlighted, there does not yet exist robust alignment in the selection-education-assignment pathway. This implies that there is an existing gap for DoD to enact the JCS vision more fully for force development. Ultimately, this will involve defining selection, education, and utilization processes more precisely for the services. If the aim is greater lethality and ingenuity through PME, the services can begin to model selection processes for additional schooling based on that principle, rather than simply sending individuals to check a box. Moreover, greater engagement with the utilization process could go a long way in improving the strength of connection between what officers and enlisted personnel learn during their time in school and the kind of work to which they are assigned upon graduation. Of course, a first step for improving that connection will be to understand the degree to which PME skills are currently utilized in the field. Given that, as the data collection process revealed, there is minimal evaluation when it comes to successful utilization of skills learned in the PME process, a clear opportunity exists to ascertain the current state of play with respect to utilization. If it turns out that utilization rates are high, there will be less work for DoD to do in order to more fully enact the CJSC vision; however, if utilization rates are low, this will be a signal that more could be done to bring PME into greater alignment with force development.

There are niche communities that do capitalize on PME experiences in graduate assignments, especially from technical schools and higher-level strategy programs, such as the Strategic Thinkers Program, JAWS, SAMS, SAASS, MAWS, and SAW.

For the broader community of officers, the services could give more attention to how they develop PME as a process that functionally—not just theoretically—prepares students for future assignments *and subsequently places them in those assignments for which they are most prepared.*

Measuring Successful Performance in the Future

An important question, related to the one above, that is not fully addressed by the JCS vision is how success should be measured. While the vision clearly is focused on outcomes-based education, an effective set of measurement tools has not yet been developed for evaluating the quality or success of PME. Putting greater definition around what "lethality and ingenuity" should look like in practice, as well as what qualifies as meaningful utilization of learned skills, is a potential path for better understanding what success looks like to the CJCS in practice. This, in turn, will better equip the institutions and the services to make necessary adjustments to better meet the needs of DoD and the combatant commands. Again, though, much of the decisionmaking around definitions of success depends on what the CJCS and DoD specifically desire from PME. If, as they state, greater alignment between selection, management, and utilization is truly desired, there remain several important steps to achieve this vision.

CHAPTER 6

Opportunities for System Enhancement

The military educational institutions share many features with their civilian counterparts in terms of how they admit and graduate students, the methods they use for teaching, and the ways they manage their faculty. But there are important differences. Civilian institutions operate in wide-ranging markets with students coming to them from many sources and taking jobs across a large range of employers. The military institutions, by contrast, operate within the specific personnel development system of DoD and its services.

To conclude this report, we offer our reflections in two areas. We discuss the topics Congress asked specifically about in Section 576 of the 2021 NDAA. These topics, presented at the beginning of the report in Box 1.1, are again presented here, along with summarized thoughts to guide readers interested in particular topic areas. We also discuss the PME system more generally in the context of this current research effort.

Admissions and Graduation

The clearest differences between military and civilian educational institutions are in student admissions. Civilian institutions dedicate significant resources to recruiting and selecting their students. In contrast, military institutions are not resourced or staffed for this responsibility, and, therefore, the role is largely borne by the services' talent management processes. For technical military education institutions, the schools do review candidate files to determine whether the officers are prepared to undertake the rigorous technical course of study, in a similar fashion to civilian universities. The services did not express a need to change these approaches.

There are clear reasons for differences in admissions approaches between military and civilian graduate schools. We think that making the admissions of military institutions more like those of civilian institutions would increase costs for the review of applications without significant benefits because these institutions must operate within the service talent management structures.

In terms of graduation, both the military and civilian schools we reviewed graduate essentially all students, and all offer similar and significant remediation programs to students who are not on track to meet graduation requirements. We observed little interest in changing these practices, and we do not see significant benefits to doing so. Making

1. Review and assess the potential effects . . . on the military education provided by the 13 DoD educational institutions: (a) Modification of **admission and graduation requirements**.

graduation from military schools easier would lessen the potential benefit of the education to each student. Making it harder could limit the number of officers graduating successfully without a clear benefit in educational terms.

The military schools in this study currently offer master's (and, in some cases, Ph.D.) degrees either automatically as part of a PME program or as an option for students who volunteer to complete additional work, such as a thesis. These degrees are seen as valuable to officers in their professional development and as signals of the wider value of military education. Reducing these opportunities would limit these positive values without any significant benefits that we can identify. Because almost all the institutions offer degrees where programs are of sufficient level and duration, we do not identify any need to change degree offerings fundamentally. Over time, additional degree options may become available as curricula change and develop.

1.(c) Reduction or expansion of degree-granting authority.

Faculty Management, Teaching Methods, and the Role of Research

1.(i) Modification of civilian faculty management practices, including employment practices.

Military schools use a variety of approaches to manage their civilian faculty. Like civilian institutions, some offer civilian faculty tenure; others appoint civilians to renewable terms. Because these terms are reportedly renewed routinely, there may be only small differences in the employment experience across these different institutions. Offering tenure may enable military institutions to compete better for civilian faculty against civilian institutions that offer it, although our discussions did not indicate that institutions using the term system see a meaningful advantage for such a change in managing civilian faculty.

1.(h) Expansion of visiting or adjunct faculty.

The military institutions also differ in their employment of adjunct and visiting faculty, which are used routinely in graduate education at civilian universities. Some military institutions, especially those with a technical focus, employ adjuncts to tap into expertise that their full-time faculty lack. Some of the strategic/operational-focused institutions have arrangements with civilian agencies to sponsor visiting faculty from these agencies, depending on the institutions' connections to these agencies. Even though some military institutions use adjunct and visiting faculty on a regular basis, others use them more sparingly. Institutions that are not currently using these faculty regularly might gain benefits from expanding opportunities for adjunct and visiting faculty or making other arrangements for their participation from related agencies.

Opportunity: **Explore additional opportunities for adjunct and visiting faculty to bring expertise, currency, and relationships with important components and agencies. Such faculty would provide greater flexibility and could help institutions address changing topics, such as the Chairman's Special Areas of Emphasis and other emerging topics.**

1.(f) Modification of military personnel career milestones in order to prioritize instructor positions.

Military educational institutions typically are seeking high-quality officers for their respective faculty billets (often including post-command, recent operational experience, and/or further promotion potential). The demand for such high-quality officers far exceeds service inventories. Representatives of military schools generally think that, over the past several years, services have not valued teaching positions as career enhancing (and individuals may share this perception).

Making major changes to service assignment policies to prioritize instructor positions might increase the qualifications of some instructors, and the services (and individuals) would likely see limitations on how they could employ their highest-quality officers.

Rather than making such significant changes, we see some modest changes that may have beneficial effects with fewer concerns. Specifically, officers currently do not receive joint credit experience for teaching at their own service institution, even though they would receive such credit for the same role at a joint or sister service institution. Addressing this policy difference for individuals teaching a joint curriculum provides an opening to signal greater service valuing of faculty assignments and may incentivize high-quality officers to consider an academic assignment more seriously.

Opportunity: **Consider granting joint assignment credit for military faculty at senior institutions, even within their own service, to promote the value of faculty assignments.**

1.(g) Increase in educational and performance requirements for military personnel selected to be instructors.

Military schools combine civilian and military faculty, each of which bring capabilities to the mix. Civilian faculty typically hold advanced degrees and provide long-term continuity and conceptual underpinnings for instruction. Military faculty bring current operational experience and therefore do not require the same level of academic education as the civilian faculty. Raising educational requirements for military faculty would likely worsen the concern described above about disincentives for the highest-quality officers to enter teaching assignments. Similarly, increasing performance requirements would narrow the pool of potential officers for these assignments and deepen the existing tensions with the services' assignment processes.

1.(b) Expansion of use of case studies in curricula for professional military education.

We find that military institutions employ a variety of instructional methods to develop their students' skills. Strategic/operational institutions, in particular, rely on case studies to develop critical analytic and decisionmaking skills and to understand historical, social, and technical contexts. Because case studies are less suited to developing specific technical skills, technical institutions tend to use them less. From the evidence developed in this study, we do not see benefits from significant expansion of case studies in either institutional type.

1.(d) Reduction or expansion of the acceptance of research grants.

The role of faculty research in military institutions is typically positioned to complement faculty teaching responsibilities. Faculty and administrators viewed the relationship between teaching and research as synergistic, and not as an explicit trade-off. Often, research efforts ensure that contemporary materials are incorporated into instruction and that students can hone critical thinking and analytical skills through independent research initiatives. Thus, we noted positive benefits for both faculty members in their continued professional development and students in their involvement in independent, high-value experiential learning. We did not observe any adverse effects associated with the balance between teaching and research commitments and expect that administrators can best manage this issue within the mission and cultural uniqueness of their respective institutions.

In some cases, external research grants can be important enablers of research activity. We observe this primarily in the technical institutions, where maintaining or expanding authority to accept grants is likely to advance the educational missions of these institutions. Strategic/operational institutions focus much less on major research projects, so the scope for accepting external grants is smaller. Even at strategic/operational institutions, there may be occasional opportunities to accept a research grant that is clearly supportive of the school's educational mission. Policies that allow acceptance of grants thus offer potential benefits even to strategic/operational institutions. As long as grants are accepted in support of the schools' primary educational missions, we see little risk to accepting them.

Effectiveness and Sizing of PME

PME institutions tend to be stable, offering programs consistently over time. Our discussions with the services indicate that they are generally satisfied with the current PME offerings and have opportunities to influence institutions to develop and modify programs when national security requirements change. For example, schools have responded to new military goals and missions by opening or expanding colleges that concentrate on cyberspace, the needs of the Space Force, and the pivot to focus on peer competitors. The coronavirus pandemic provided opportunities for institutions to show agility and responsiveness by modifying their delivery means to reach service members who could not attend class in person. The OBME approach adopted in the recent JCS Vision could further clarify how national security outcomes drive the goals and missions of PME institutions. Consistent with the OBME approach, the Joint Staff's vision for PME is evolving beyond topical areas required for compliance with statute and toward meeting the challenges posed by adversaries in an era of strategic competition. As a result, they are calling for PME institutions to increase their classified capabilities and facilities.

PME institutions operate in the talent management context set by the services, which poses challenges to utilizing graduates and providing feedback to educational institutions.

Services and schools repeatedly reported that postgraduation assignments often do not build on the skills that graduates learn during their PME experiences. This disparity has been consistently reported and is also a source of frustration for military students. However, there are niche communities that do capitalize on PME experiences in graduate assignments, specifically technical schools and higher-level strategy

3. Assess the requirements of the **goals and missions** of the 13 DoD educational institutions and any need to adjust such goals and missions to **meet national security requirements** of the DoD.

4. Assess the **effectiveness and shortfalls** of the existing professional military education enterprise as measured **against graduate utilization, postgraduate evaluations, and the education and force development requirements** of the Chairman of the Joint Chiefs of Staff and the Chiefs of the Armed Forces.

programs. The JCS Vision calls for more of this type of integrated PME and talent management.

Opportunity: **Build on service talent management efforts in specialized areas that have had success in better matching PME graduates' skills to assignment opportunities.**

The OBME approach calls for decisions on curricula and teaching methods to be informed by signals of demand and graduate outcomes. Military schools expressed strong support for this vision but noted that they face significant challenges in getting actionable information from the services and joint community to make these decisions. Such information could include systematic analysis of graduate performance in future assignments and structured feedback from commanders on knowledge and skills needed in those assignments.

Opportunity: **Develop better signals of demand and value from the services and joint community to inform school curriculum decisions relative to expected outcomes required of graduates.**

Because of these limitations related to (1) the lack of clear performance expectations demanded of graduates to be successful in follow-on assignments, (2) close alignment of graduates to billets that require their education, and (3) analysis of graduate performance in their future assignments, it is difficult to systematically and objectively measure the effectiveness of PME.

1.(e) Reduction or expansion of the **number of attending students** generally.

The services did not indicate significant need or interest in either increasing or decreasing the number of officers attending PME. The general perception was that the educational system produced sufficient numbers of graduates to address service and joint needs, but this specific issue had not been systematically studied by the services.

1.(j) Reduction of the number of attending students through the sponsoring of education of an **increased number of students at non-DoD institutions** of higher education.

The Navy did express an alternative perspective in that it is compelled to provide officers to the JPME system because a mix of students from every service is required to meet joint policy requirements (as well as for diversity among service officers who are to become faculty). In its view, the Navy could use its officers more efficiently by sending fewer of them to JPME and reserving more of them for operational naval assignments. Because of the statutory requirements for a mix of joint representation in both students and faculty, the Navy representatives find that it is consistently difficult to satisfy both their service and joint requirements for educated and experienced officers.

Congress asked whether students could attend civilian institutions instead of PME institutions. Many officers do attend civilian graduate programs, and these experiences can play valuable roles in officer development. However, civilian offerings cannot devote the attention to federal and DoD policy and strategy that officers require in their military leadership roles. The services value civilian graduate education when it develops specialized capabilities that are not common enough to justify developing a military-specific education program.

Civilian programs generally do not satisfy JPME requirements that are needed for any officers to be considered for promotion to flag or general officer, although the U.S. Space Force is currently pursuing a combined civilian-military program that meets JPME requirements. The service is developing this program with JHU SAIS. Working with the JPME oversight organizations, the service is seeking to comply with the requisite congressional and policy requirements to ensure that civilian offerings and their graduates will be designated as joint qualified. Complying with these joint requirements is no small feat, but pursuing this objective is consistent with the flexibility needed in a modern talent management system. Note that the enhancement opportunities detailed above also apply to new educational alternatives. The U.S. Space Force innovation in educational delivery offers a valuable opportunity to monitor and assess this experience and to determine whether it holds lessons that can be applied more broadly. Accordingly, formative and summative evaluations should be an explicit design feature of the JHU SAIS program. Such evaluations can inform future decisions on whether some of the present demand met by military educational institutions could realistically be met by civilian institutions, with or without relief from congressional statutes or joint policy requirements.

Conclusion

Congress asked fundamental questions regarding the role, conduct, and management of PME in DoD. In our research, the services largely expressed satisfaction with the alignment of military educational institutions with their mission needs, although the Navy would prefer to lighten the involvement of its officers in JPME. We found that technical institutions naturally focus on more technical content and have a more direct style of instruction. In contrast, strategic/operational institutions cover broader topics and more frequently use techniques (such as case studies) that allow students to appreciate complex interactions, past lessons, and applications to future uncertainties. Technical institutions have important input into student selection, and their graduates often are placed into relevant follow-on assignments. Strategic/operational institutions, on the other hand, receive students selected by the services to meet talent management goals, and the relation of follow-on assignments can be unclear.

We identified several opportunities for enhancing the DoD educational system and its supporting processes. The schools and services would benefit from clearer expressions of demand that schools can use to guide development of curricula and adoption of teaching methods. The services can build on existing talent management efforts in specialized areas by increasing the overall match between PME graduates' educational outcomes and subsequent assignment opportunities. Although we found that some schools use a variety of adjunct and visiting faculty, others show little or no use of these options. We think that all schools should assess their opportunities to use such faculty to expand their educational capabilities and stakeholder networks in support of meeting mission demands.

Based on these analyses, this chapter provided a specific response to each issue that Congress raised in Section 576.

DoD Educational Institution Profiles

Strategic/Operational Institutions

AIR UNIVERSITY (PME COMPONENTS)[1]

Air University (AU) operates the Department of the Air Force (DAF) (Air Force and Space Force) PME enterprise at Maxwell Air Force Base, Alabama, and AFIT at Wright-Patterson Air Force Base, Ohio (Figure A.1). AU's officer education components include the following:

- **Air Command and Staff College** (ACSC) provides DAF intermediate developmental education and JPME-I in the Master of Military Operational Art and Science degree program for field-grade officers.
- **Air War College** (AWC) provides DAF senior developmental education and JPME-II in the Master of Strategic Studies degree program for senior field-grade officers.

FIGURE A.1

Air University "Props and Wings" Monument

---

[1] Information in this section is derived from AU's responses to the project's requests for information and Air University, homepage, undated.

- **Air Force Institute of Technology** (AFIT) provides professional continuing education and accredited graduate degrees (master and doctorate) in a range of technical and engineering fields. It is described fully under the Technical Institutions section later in this appendix.
- **The Curtis E. LeMay Center for Doctrine Development and Education** develops warfighters for the joint and combined team through doctrine, education, and wargaming.
- **The Ira C. Eaker Center for Professional Development** provides functionally aligned technical training and professional continuing education.
- **The Squadron Officer College** provides primary developmental education for company-grade DAF officers.
- **The International Officer School** provides international military officers with preparatory programs for each of the resident officer PME programs.
- **The School of Advanced Air and Space Studies (SAASS)** provides select graduates of intermediate developmental education programs with an opportunity for further advanced education to develop strategists for the DAF. SAASS is the DAF element of DoD's advanced studies group program.

AU's administrative and educational support units include the following:

- **The Chief Academic Officer and Office of Academic and Faculty Affairs** provides oversight and administrative control over educational programs at AU.
- **HQ AU/A-3, Academic Operations,** provides administrative and operational support to all educational and administrative support programs throughout AU.
- **The Teaching and Learning Center** provides services in faculty development, writing support, and educational technology training (educational support).
- **The Office of AU Registrar** represents the institution in ensuring the accuracy and integrity of the academic records for all students (administrative support).

- **Air University Press** publishes scholarly books, journals, faculty research, student papers selected by AU schools, and other administrative documents for AU (educational support).
- **The Office of Sponsored Programs** "facilitates projects between AU organizations and external sponsors, ranging from formalized Research Task Forces and media like the Wild Blue Yonder blog and podcast to one-off requests for expertise, coordination, and event planning" (educational support).[2]
- **The AU Innovation Accelerator** connects AU faculty, staff, and students with partners in DoD, academia, and industry, identifying opportunities for collaboration and for developing new capabilities, strategies, and technologies (educational support).
- **The Muir S. Fairchild Research and Information Center (also known as the AU Library)** directly connects and collaborates on efforts of library collection development, instruction, and curriculum through the maintenance of a substantial print book collection, electronic resources, and the Innovation Lab (educational support).

AU also includes other components that address enlisted education, officer accessions, test pilot training, and traditional support units (e.g., finance, legal).

Below, we provide details for ACSC and AWC. AFIT is discussed in the subsection on technical institutions.

AIR COMMAND AND STAFF COLLEGE

Educational focus: The Air Command and Staff College (ACSC) is the intermediate-level PME institution for the Air Force and Space Force. ACSC teaches the skills necessary to conduct air, space, and cyberspace operations in support of joint warfighting and multi-domain campaigns.

Research centers: ACSC incorporates research into its educational activities and does not have dedicated research centers.

Degree programs: Master of Military Operational Art and Science. JPME-I credit for U.S. officers. Ten-month in-residence education or self-paced (up to five years) online education. Online program is taught by separate faculty.

Non-degree programs and other activities: ACSC provides an online non-degree program in addition to its online degree program. It offers JPME-I credit for U.S. officers.

Admission standards: Students are selected to attend in residence by a central selection board. To enroll, officers are required to (1) possess a qualifying undergraduate degree or meet alternate academic credentials admission requirements and (2) provide an acceptable score on the Test of English as a Foreign Language (TOEFL) if they are not from an English-speaking country.

Graduation standards: Complete the 30-semester-hour ACSC resident program. Students must achieve a grade of C or higher on each academic course with an overall GPA of 3.00 on a 4.00 scale and dem-

---

[2] Air University, "Office of Sponsored Programs (OSP)," webpage, undated.

onstrate fully satisfactory participation in other scheduled ACSC programs and activities to earn the master's degree. Failure to graduate is rare.

Faculty appointment practices: Military faculty typically rotate in and out every three or four years. Civilian faculty operate in a reappointment system.

External funding: None.

AIR WAR COLLEGE

Educational focus: Air War College (AWC) is the senior-level PME institution for the Air Force and Space Force. AWC educates senior military officers and civilians to serve as critical and strategic thinkers and enables them to serve as national security senior leaders.

Degree programs: Master of Strategic Studies. Ten-month in-residence education. JPME-II credit for U.S. officers.

Non-degree programs and other activities:

- **AWC** provides an online non-degree PME program. It offers JPME-II credit for U.S. officers.
- **The Air Force Cyber College** is the cyber knowledge, education, and research center for the Air Force and national leaders.
- **The Air Force Culture and Language Center** provides language, regional expertise, and culture education to enhance interoperability and build partner capacity across the spectrum of military operations.
- **The Air Force Negotiations Center** develops negotiation capability as a critical, engaged-leadership competency across DoD.
- **The Center for Strategy and Technology** (also known as Blue Horizons) offers meta-strategy for the Age of Surprise.
- **The Center for Strategic Deterrence Studies** develops Air Force, DoD, and other U.S. government leaders to advance the state of knowledge, policy, and practices within strategic defense issues involving nuclear, biological, and chemical weapons.

Admission standards: The Central Senior Service School Selection Board, Headquarters U.S. Air Force, selects Air Force active-duty officers to attend AWC. To enroll, officers are required to (1) possess a qualifying undergraduate degree or academic credentials requirements through a foreign credential evaluation and (2) provide an acceptable score on the TOEFL if they are not from an English-speaking country.

Graduation standards: Complete 35 or 36 semester credits. Students must achieve a grade of B or higher on each academic course with an overall GPA of at least 3.00 on a 4.00 scale, achieve a "pass" in the Global Challenge Wargame, and fully participate in the National Security Forum and Commandant's Lecture Series. International Fellows receiving the diploma participate in core and elective courses, the Global Challenge Wargame, the National Security Forum, and the Commandant's Lecture Series. Students earning the diploma may enroll in a research course. Core courses completed for the diploma are graded on a pass/fail basis; elective courses are taken in an audit status. Failure to graduate is rare.

Faculty appointment practices: Military faculty typically rotate in and out every three or four years. Civilian faculty operate in a reappointment system.

External funding: Less than $10,000 in faculty travel is annually funded by private entities.

See Tables A.1–A.5.

TABLE A.1

ACSC Enrolled Students

	ACSC ONLINE NON-DEGREE				ACSC ONLINE DEGREE				ACSC IN-RESIDENCE NON-DEGREE				ACSC IN-RESIDENCE DEGREE			
	2019	2020	2021	2022	2019	2020	2021	2022	2019	2020	2021	2022	2019	2020	2021	2022
U.S. Army	0	1	2	1	2	3	3	6	0	0	0	0	45	45	40	39
U.S. Navy	239	544	498	515	19	35	46	120	0	0	0	0	14	14	12	4
U.S. Marine Corps	71	164	148	188	8	10	18	38	0	0	0	0	12	12	12	12
U.S. Air Force	1,890	3,350	2,760	3,752	489	674	304	1,779	0	0	0	0	326	324	333	334
U.S. Space Force	0	0	59	133	0	0	9	70	0	0	0	0	0	0	0	23
U.S. Coast Guard	27	64	66	53	7	11	20	55	0	0	0	0	1	1	1	1
Foreign military	17	24	18	41	0	0	0	0	55	49	53	62	23	26	11	80
DoD civilian	307	394	401	483	177	200	148	49	0	0	0	0	23	19	21	14
Other civilian	8	10	0	2	13	11	10	12	0	0	0	0	0	0	0	4
Total students enrolled	2,559	4,551	3,952	5,168	715	944	558	2,129	55	49	53	62	444	441	430	511

SOURCE: AU response to request for information.

TABLE A.2

AWC Enrolled Students

	AWC ONLINE NON-DEGREE				AWC IN-RESIDENCE NON-DEGREE				AWC IN-RESIDENCE DEGREE			
	2019	2020	2021	2022	2019	2020	2021	2022	2019	2020	2021	2022
U.S. Army	17	14	14	8	0	0	0	0	37	37	37	35
U.S. Navy	2	14	11	2	0	0	0	0	7	5	3	2
U.S. Marine Corps	121	132	105	128	0	0	0	0	9	10	9	9
U.S. Air Force	2,136	2,363	1,606	1,869	0	0	0	0	115	120	102	105
U.S. Space Force	0	0	60	43	0	0	0	0	0	0	6	9
U.S. Coast Guard	2	2	4	2	0	0	0	0	1	1	1	1
Foreign military	5	3	2	2	32	28	28	31	13	16	9	46
DoD civilian	600	496	368	109	0	0	0	0	18	14	15	13
Other civilian	4	5	2	15	0	0	0	0	9	9	4	5
Total students enrolled	2,887	3,029	2,172	2,178	32	28	28	31	209	212	186	225

SOURCE: AU response to request for information.

TABLE A.3

ACSC and AWC Faculty

	ACSC ONLINE FACULTY		ACSC IN-RESIDENCE FACULTY		AWC FACULTY		AWC AND ACSC TOTAL FACULTY	
	FULL TIME	PART TIME[a]	FULL TIME	PART TIME	FULL TIME	PART TIME	FULL TIME	PART TIME
DoD military officers	16	0	61	17	31	2	108	19
DoD civilians	30	0	49	8	29	15	108	23
Other U.S. government civilians	0	0	0	0	3	0	3	0
Other civilians	0	238	0	0	0	0	0	238
Enlisted	7	0	0	0	0	0	7	0
International military officers	0	0	4	0	2	0	6	0
Total	53	238	114	25	65	17	232	280

SOURCE: AU response to request for information.
[a] ACSC online part-time faculty represents the total number of part-time contractor faculty rather than FTEs.

TABLE A.4

ACSC and AWC Staff (non-faculty)

	AWC STAFF		ACSC STAFF		AWC AND ACSC TOTAL STAFF	
	FULL TIME	PART TIME	FULL TIME	PART TIME	FULL TIME	PART TIME
DoD military officers	16	8	8	0	24	8
DoD civilians	37	23	12	0	49	23
Other U.S. government civilians	0	0	0	0	0	0
Other civilians	13	0	0	0	13	0
Enlisted	8	4	3	0	11	4
International military officers	0	0	0	0	0	0
Total	74	35	23	0	97	35

SOURCE: AU response to request for information.

TABLE A.5

AU Expenditures, FY 2019—2021 ($ millions)

	FY 2019	FY 2020	FY 2021	FY 2022
ACSC				
Military personnel	$14.1	$14.2	$13.8	$17.0
Civilian personnel	$11.7	$13.2	$13.8	$14.0
Operations and maintenance	$9.0	$9.5	$9.8	$9.9
Total	$34.8	$36.9	$37.4	$40.9
AWC				
Military personnel	$8.2	$8.0	$7.5	$7.7
Civilian personnel	$9.5	$9.3	$11.2	$10.4
Operations and maintenance	$4.2	$3.4	$4.4	$5.0
Total	$22.0	$20.7	$23.1	$23.1

SOURCE: AU response to request for information.

U.S. ARMY COMMAND AND GENERAL STAFF COLLEGE[3]

The main campus of the U.S. Army Command and General Staff College (CGSC) is located in Fort Leavenworth, Kansas, and is home to three different schools (Figure A.2). A fourth school is located on a branch campus in Fort Bliss, Texas. Each is described in the following section, along with further information about graduation and admission standards, academic programs, faculty, student enrollment, and budget.

Educational focus: The mission of the CGSC is to "educate, train, and develop leaders for Unified Land Operations in a Joint, interagency, intergovernmental, and multinational operational environment; and to advance the art and science of the Profession of Arms in support of Army operational requirements."[4]

Major organizational units:

CGSC maintains four schools:

- The **Command and General Staff School** delivers a ten-month Command and General Staff Officers Course (CGSOC) in residence at Fort Leavenworth, Kansas, to U.S. military officers, international military officers, and interagency partners. The school also teaches the CGSOC Common Core to students at two satellite campuses and teaches the CGSOC Common Core and Advanced Operations Course via distance learning to active and reserve component officers around the world.
- The **School of Advanced Military Studies** (SAMS) provides the Advanced Military Studies Program for officers and the Advanced

FIGURE A.2

Eisenhower Hall, Fort Leavenworth, Kansas

---

[3] Information in this section is derived from CGSG's responses to the project's requests for information and Command and General Staff College, "Command and General Staff College (CGSC)," webpage, undated.

[4] U.S. Army, "CGSC Circular 350-1: U.S. Army Command and General Staff College Catalog," 2016, pp. 1–2.

Strategic Leadership Studies Program for a select number of U.S. officers, international officers, and U.S. agency partners. The Advanced Strategic Leadership Studies Program offers JPME-II credit.

- The **School for Command Preparation** provides continuing education for future Army battalion and brigade commanders, command sergeants major, and spouses in ten one- to four-week courses offered multiple times during each academic year.
- The **Sergeants Major Academy** in Fort Bliss, Texas, offers the ten-month Sergeants Major Course-Resident to senior U.S. and international noncommissioned officers and offers the Sergeants Major Course via distance learning to mainly Army Reserve and National Guard noncommissioned officers around the world.

CGSC administration includes three primary support units. The largest support element is the **CGSC Office of the Dean of Academics**. The second support unit is the **Commandant's Distinguished Chairs**. Coming from the Central Intelligence Agency (CIA), State Department, Defense Intelligence Agency (DIA), United States Agency for International Development (USAID), Space and Missile Command, and the Ike Skelton Chair for Art of War Scholars, these individuals are college-level faculty serving academic programs in all four schools. The third support unit, under the CGSC Dean of Academics, is the **Ike Skelton Combined Arms Research Library**, which serves CGSC resident and distance learning students, the Fort Leavenworth community, and researchers across DoD.

Degree programs: CGSC receives its degree-granting authority from Title 10 U.S. Code Section 7414 and from CGSC's regional accrediting body, the Higher Learning Commission. CGSC offers four master's degrees, one bachelor's degree, and one undergraduate-level certificate.

- The *Master in Military Art and Science* is an in-residence CGSOC program focused on producing researchers through the actual conduct and writing of research and with the goal to create research products (theses) of value to the military profession and associated disciplines.
- The *Master in Operational Studies* is a practitioner's degree with emphasis on the knowledge, skills, and attributes essential for officers at the higher tactical and operational levels of conflict.
- Graduates of SAMS's Advanced Military Studies Program receive a *Master of Arts in Military Operations*.
- Graduates of SAMS's Advanced Strategic Leadership Studies Program earn a *Master of Arts in Strategic Studies*. JPME-II credit is awarded to U.S. officers.
- Sergeants Major Course students may pursue a *B.A. in Leadership and Workforce Development*.

Completion of the CGSOC grants JPME-I credit to U.S. officers.

Non-degree programs and other activities: Resident and distance learning Sergeants Major Course students who meet all program requirements earn a CGSC undergraduate-level certificate in Leadership and Workforce Development.

Admissions standards: The school itself does not ultimately play a role in determining which students attend. Selection is handled by centralized boards for the Department of the Army. In many cases, admission is based not on academic prowess but rather on military record. There are some minimum requirements, however. Every admitted student in a CGSC master's degree program must have previously earned an accredited bachelor's degree or international equivalent. Full admission to the Master in Military Art and Science program depends on submission of an approved research prospectus, an application, and transcripts (if required) and successful completion of a Research Methods or Historical Research Methods elective.

Graduation standards: Each degree program has different graduation requirements.

- In the *Master in Military Art and Science* program, students write and defend an approved research thesis, complete the CGSOC curriculum, and pass an oral defense of the thesis. Furthermore, a Master in Military Art and Science candidate must earn a B or better on all CGSOC coursework; should a student earn a C or below in any course, they are disenrolled from the Master in Military Art and Science program.
- In the *Master in Operational Studies* program, degree candidates must complete all CGSOC coursework and established assessments, earning a B or better for all transcript-reportable items. In the resident course, roughly 10 percent of a class goes on probation for academic performance reasons; roughly ten to 15 of approximately 1,200 students will not pass the course.
- In the *Master of Arts in Military Operations* program, degree candidates must complete all Advanced Military Studies Program coursework with a B or better, write a publishable monograph of 10,000 words or longer under the supervision of SAMS faculty, and pass an oral comprehensive examination.
- In the *Master of Arts in Strategic Studies* program, degree candidates must complete all Advanced Strategic Leadership Studies Program coursework with a B or better, write a publishable research monograph of 10,000 words or more, and pass an oral comprehensive examination.
- *B.A. in Leadership and Workforce Development* degree candidates must complete all Sergeants Major Course coursework with a grade of C or better, achieve a cumulative GPA of at least 2.0 for all Leadership and Workforce Development courses, and graduate from the Sergeants Major Course.

Faculty appointment practices: There is no tenure for CGSC faculty. Civilian faculty are hired on one- to five-year appointments that can be renewed for two to five years, and they make up roughly 60 to 65 percent of all faculty. Reappointments are generally granted, but not always, and are based on performance. There are no adjunct faculty. Military faculty rotate every two or three years and make up roughly 35 to 40 percent of all faculty.

External funding: CGSC does not have the legislative authority to accept research grants. External support for faculty positions does exist, but only through memoranda of understanding with U.S. governmental agencies, including CIA, the State Department, USAID, the U.S. Army

Space and Missile Defense Command, and DIA. These five memoranda of understanding have resulted in one faculty member per agency for the past two years.

See Tables A.6–A.8.

TABLE A.6

CGSC Students Enrolled, 2019—2022

	CGSC RESIDENT DEGREE PROGRAMS				CGSC NON-RESIDENT DEGREE PROGRAMS				NON-RESIDENT CERTIFICATE/ NON-DEGREE SEEKING			
	2019	2020	2021	2022	2019	2020	2021	2022	2019	2020	2021	2022
U.S. Army	1,133	1,307	1,214	1,186	0	0	0	0	0	0	0	229
U.S. Navy	28	23	25	20	0	0	0	0	0	0	0	0
U.S. Marine Corps	32	40	40	39	0	0	0	0	0	0	0	2
U.S. Air Force	91	82	82	87	0	0	0	0	0	0	0	0
U.S. Coast Guard	3	3	2	4	0	0	0	0	0	0	0	1
U.S. Space Force	0	0	0	2	0	0	0	0	0	0	0	n/a
International military	139	154	77	151	0	0	0	0	0	0	0	32
DoD civilian	13	12	0	0	0	0	0	0	0	0	0	0
Other civilian	19	12	12	14	0	0	0	0	0	0	0	0
Total	1,458	1,633	1,452	1,503	0	0	0	0	0	0	0	264

SOURCE: CGSC response to request for information.
NOTE: n/a = not applicable.

TABLE A.7

CGSC Personnel (as of October 2021)

	RESIDENT FACULTY		NON-RESIDENT FACULTY		STAFF	
	FULL TIME	PART TIME (FTE)	FULL TIME	PART TIME (FTE)	FULL TIME	PART TIME (FTE)
DoD military officers	133	6.6	33	0	19	0
DoD military enlisted	45	0.6	26	0	1	0
DoD civilians	230	12.0	83	0	101	0
Other civilians	4	2.7	0	0	0	0
International military officers	15	0.0	0	0	0	0
Total	427	21.9	142	0	121	0

SOURCE: CGSC response to request for information.
NOTE: Part-time faculty FTE numbers are rounded to one decimal place.

TABLE A.8

CGSC Expenditures, FY 2019—2022 ($ millions)

	FY 2019	FY 2020	FY 2021	FY 2022
Military personnel	295.9	311.2	313.76	316.13
Civilian personnel	109.5	116.2	110.3	116.91
Operations and maintenance	71.4	59.1	46.6	47.65
Total	476.8	486.5	470.6	480.7

SOURCE: CGSC response to request for information.
NOTE: Columns may not add to exact totals because of rounding.

U.S. Army War College[5]

The U.S. Army War College (USAWC), in Carlisle, Pennsylvania, houses one school, three research and wargaming centers, and one program for general officer education (Figure A.3). Each is described in this section, along with further information about graduation and admission standards, academic programs, faculty, student enrollment, and budget.

Educational focus: The mission of USAWC is "to enhance national and global security by developing ideas and educating U.S. and international leaders to serve and lead at the strategic-enterprise level."[6]

Major organizational units:

USAWC maintains one school:

- The **School of Strategic Landpower** develops strategic leaders by providing a strong foundation of wisdom grounded in mastery of the profession of arms and by serving as a crucible for educating future leaders in the analysis, evaluation, and refinement of professional expertise in war, strategy, operations, national security, resource management, and responsible command.[7]
- USAWC maintains three research and wargaming centers:
- The **Center for Strategic Leadership** develops senior leaders and supports the strategic needs of the Army by educating senior military and civilian leaders on land power at the operational and strategic levels; developing expert knowledge and solutions for the operating and generating forces; and conducting research activities, strategic exercises, and strategic communication.[8]
- The **Strategic Studies Institute** "conducts geostrategic research and analysis that creates and advances knowledge and solutions for national security challenges facing the Army."[9] The Strategic

---

[5] Information in this section is derived from USAWC's responses to the project's requests for information and U.S. Army War College, homepage, undated.

[6] Lawanda Warthen, "The U.S. Army War College Breaks New Ground in Hybrid Education," Army.mil, 2021.

[7] Robert J. Bunker, "Armed Robotic Systems Emergence: Weapons Systems Life Cycles Analysis and New Strategic Realities," U.S. Army War College, 2017, p. i.

[8] U.S. Army War College, "Center for Strategic Leadership," webpage, undated.

[9] Strategic Studies Institute, "Our Mission," webpage, undated.

FIGURE A.3

U.S. Army War College, Main Entrance, Carlisle, Pennsylvania

Studies Institute supports the Army Staff and joint and Army major commands by "analyzing critical issues and publishing findings and recommendations to inform" senior defense leaders and their staffs.[10]

- The **U.S. Army Heritage and Education Center** "acquires, conserves, and exhibits historical materials for use to support the U.S. Army, educate an international audience, and honor soldiers—past and present."[11]
- The **Army Strategic Education Program** is an executive-level education program executing General Officer PME for the entire population of Army General Officers. Programs last from one to three weeks. Participants must pass graded events in Advanced and Nominative Leader Course programs, as well as attend and participate in all required courses.

USAWC administration includes the offices of the commandant, provost, deputy commandant, chief of staff, and command sergeant major.

Degree programs: USAWC offers three academic degree programs:

- The *Resident Senior Service College* is an in-residence program resulting in a Master of Strategic Studies degree and senior service college diploma. The program lasts ten months and grants JPME-II credit.
- The *Distance Joint Studies Program* is a remote program resulting in a Master of Strategic Studies degree and senior service college diploma. The program lasts two years and grants JPME-II credit.
- The *Distance Senior Service College* is a remote program resulting in a Master of Strategic Studies degree and senior service college diploma. The program lasts two years and grants JPME-I credit.

---

10 Strategic Studies Institute, undated.

11 U.S. Army Heritage and Education Center," Visit Us," webpage, undated.

Non-degree professional programs and other activities:

- The *USAWC Fellows Program* is a broadening program that sends students to one of 50 programs worldwide. The program lasts ten months and grants a senior service college diploma.
- The *Basic Strategic Art Program* is an in-residence program focused on developing strategic expertise for the Functional Area 59 role (i.e., U.S. Army Strategist). The program lasts ten months and operates at the intermediate level.
- USAWC offers a graduate certificate program. The *Graduate Certificate in National Security Studies* is a distance education program that helps prepare working professionals for future national security positions. Students must complete four eight-week core courses and one elective course to earn the certificate.

Admissions standards: The school itself does not play a role in determining which students attend. Beyond having a college degree, there is no minimum GPA requirement or prerequisite courses necessary for officers to be admitted; it is done so at the discretion of the service. In many cases, those officers who are admitted have excelled in tactical situations. Officers matriculated into JPME-II programs must have previously completed JPME-I education.

Graduation standards: Each degree program has different graduation requirements. In the *Basic Strategic Art Program*, students must attain a 3.0 GPA in all courses to pass. In the *Resident Senior Service College*, students must attain a 3.0 GPA in all core courses and electives; pass an oral comprehensive exam; and complete additional course requirements, such as public speaking engagements and staff rides. In the *Distance Joint Studies Program* and the *Distance Senior Service College*, students must attain a 3.0 GPA in all courses and electives to pass. In the *USAWC Fellows* program, students must pass graded events in Advanced and Nominative Leader Course programs, in addition to attending and participating in all required courses. Across all programs, failure to graduate is very rare.

Faculty appointment practices: Military faculty typically rotate in and out every three to four years. Civilian faculty operate in a reappointment system, in which they maintain their post so long as their work is satisfactory and there is a need for their skill set.

External funding: USAWC has legislative policy and departmental approval to accept external funding but is still developing local policy for accepting research grants. External funding for the past three years came from only one source, the Army War College Foundation. Funding amounts were $881,184 in FY 2019, $1,117,500 in FY 2020, and $882,610 in FY 2021.

See Tables A.9–A.11.

TABLE A.9

AWC Students Enrolled, 2019—2022

CATEGORY	USAWC RESIDENT				USAWC NON-RESIDENT				CERTIFICATE/NON-DEGREE-SEEKING			
	2019	2020	2021	2022	2019	2020	2021	2022	2019	2020	2021	2022
U.S. Army	225	225	215	222	315	315	322	293	868	581	513	883
U.S. Navy	9	9	8	10	3	3	6	10	1	0	3	0
U.S. Marine Corps	17	17	16	15	14	14	18	11	1	0	3	0
U.S. Air Force	26	26	26	24	5	5	5	17	2	0	1	0
U.S. Coast Guard	1	1	1	1	0	0	0	0	0	0	0	0
U.S. Space Force	0	0	0	2	0	0	0	0	0	0	0	0
International military	76	76	66	80	9	9	7	5	124	90	115	117
DoD civilian	28	28	33	24	24	24	10	15	70	99	18	20
Other civilian	0	0	0	0	0	0	24	27	0	0	0	141
Total	382	382	365	378	370	370	392	378	1,066	770	653	1,161

SOURCE: USAWC response to request for information.

TABLE A.10

AWC Personnel (as of November 2022)

PROGRAM AND STAFF CATEGORY	FACULTY		STAFF	
	FULL TIME	PART TIME (FTE)	FULL TIME	PART TIME (FTE)
USAWC headquarters				
DoD military officers	5	0	25	0
DoD military enlisted	0	0	4	1
DoD civilians	8	0	77	0
Other civilians	0	0	0	0
International military officers	0	0	0	0
Program total	13	0	106	1
School of Strategic Landpower				
DoD military officers	69	20	1	0
DoD military enlisted	0	0	0	0
DoD civilians	44	11	36	0
Other civilians	13	0	0	0
International military officers	3	0	0	0
Program total	129	31	37	0

Table A.10—Continued

PROGRAM AND STAFF CATEGORY	FACULTY		STAFF	
	FULL TIME	PART TIME (FTE)	FULL TIME	PART TIME (FTE)
Center for Strategic Leadership				
DoD military officers	0	0	23	16
DoD military enlisted	0	0	6	3
DoD civilians	6	7.5	50	0
Other civilians	6	0	0	0
International military officers	0	0	0	0
Program total	12	7.5	79	19
Strategic Studies Institute				
DoD military officers	0	0	6	0
DoD military enlisted	0	0	0	0
DoD civilians	14	1	13	0
Other civilians	1	0	0	0
International military officers	0	0	0	0
Program total	15	1	19	0
Army Heritage Education Center				
DoD military officers	0	0	1	6
DoD military enlisted	0	0	0	0
DoD civilians	2	1	59	0
Other civilians	0	0	0	0
International military officers	0	0	0	0
Program total	2	1	60	6
Army Strategic Education Program				
DoD military officers	0	0	2	0
DoD military enlisted	0	0	1	0
DoD civilians	0	1	10	0
Other civilians	3	20	0	0
International military officers	0	0	0	0
Program total	3	21	13	0
Grand total	174	61.5	314	26

SOURCE: USAWC response to request for information.

TABLE A.11

AWC Expenditures for FY 2019–2022 ($ millions)

CATEGORY	FY 2019	FY 2020	FY 2021	FY 2022
Military personnel	13.2	13.6	14.0	10.4
Civilian personnel	5.4	7.0	6.1	7.7
Operations and maintenance	5.5	5.6	3.9	2.9
Total	24.1	26.0	24.1	21.0

SOURCE: USAWC response to request for information.
NOTE: Columns may not add to exact totals because of rounding.

Marine Corps University[12]

Marine Corps University (MCU) operates the Marine Corps' PME enterprise at Marine Corps Base Quantico, Virginia (Figure A.4). MCU's officer education and research components include the following:

- **Command and Staff College** (CSC) provides graduate-level education and training in order to develop critical thinkers, innovative problem solvers, and ethical leaders who will serve as commanders and staff officers with Marine Air Ground Task Forces and with service, joint, interagency, intergovernmental and multinational organizations confronting complex and uncertain security environments. U.S. students (and select international students) earn MCU's Master's in Military Studies (and JPME-I credit). The CSC Resident Program educates roughly 225 students annually. MCU's College of Distance Education and Training delivers the CSC Distance and Blended Programs, which educate roughly 1,400 students annually.
- **Marine Corps War College** (MCWAR) educates selected military and civilian professionals in order to develop military strategists, critical and creative thinkers, strategic leaders, and joint warfighters, who are prepared to meet the challenges of a complex and dynamic security environment. U.S. students (and select international students) earn MCU's Masters of Strategic Studies. MCWAR educates roughly 30 students annually.
- The **School of Advanced Warfighting** (SAW) develops lead planners and future commanders to be able to design and execute joint campaigns and naval expeditionary operations. It is an 11-month post JPME-I advanced intermediate-level (O-4) PME program; students earn MCU's Masters of Operational Studies and the additional 0505 Operational Planner and 0506 Red Team Member military occupational specialties. Students do not earn JPME credit. SAW educates roughly 26 students annually.
- The **Expeditionary Warfare School** (EWS) educates company grade officers to prepare them mentally, morally, and physi-

---

[12] Information in this section is derived from MCU's responses to the project's requests for information and Marine Corps University, homepage, undated.

FIGURE A.4

U.S. Marine Corps University, Main Entrance, Quantico, Virginia

cally for billets of increased leadership responsibility. EWS resident program educates roughly 225 students annually. The College of Distance Education and Training's EWS Distance and Blended Programs educate roughly 2,100 students annually.

- The **Brute Krulak Center for Innovation and Future Warfare** engages in complex problem-solving, as well as facilitating and encouraging novel solutions to current and future warfighting challenges, to include administering MCU's educational wargaming efforts, in support of all educational programs.

MCU also includes other educational components that address enlisted education.

MCU administrative support units include the following:

- **Academic Support Division** supports the provost in the development of U.S. Marine Corps PME policy, to include assisting with JPME requirements, developing MCU academic policy, managing the curricula review process, and performing registrar functions for resident officer programs. The director serves as MCU's liaison with Southern Association of Colleges and Schools Commission on Colleges on all issues related to institutional accreditation.
- **Faculty Development and Outreach Coordinator** provides guidance on the orientation and continued professional development of faculty.
- **Institutional Research, Assessment, and Planning** provides assessment support and guidance to monitor both direct and indirect measures of achievement, academically and administratively.
- **Information Technology** Directorate plans, develops, acquires, and maintains the information and communication tools.

- **Leadership Communication Skills Center** serves as an instructional communication support center for MCU students, faculty, and staff by strengthening individuals' written and oral communication skills.
- **Comptroller's Office** provides financial management guidance and oversight to the commanding general and staff.
- **Administrative/Student Services** is responsible for all administrative requirements for the commanding general, permanent personnel, and individual mobilized assigned reservists assigned to Education Command.
- **Library of the Marine Corps** is composed of the Research Library Branch, the Virtual Library Branch, and the Quantico Base Library.

Below, we provide more-detailed information on CSC and MCWAR.

COMMAND AND STAFF COLLEGE

Educational focus: Command and Staff College (CSC) is the primary intermediate-level PME program for the Marine Corps. CSC develops critical thinkers, innovative problem-solvers, and ethical leaders who will serve as commanders and staff officers.

Research centers: CSC incorporates research into its educational activities and does not have dedicated research centers.

Degree programs: Master of Military Studies. JPME-I credit for U.S. officers. Ten-month in-residence education.

Non-degree programs and other activities: The College of Distance Education and Training provides a CSC distance non-degree program. It offers JPME-I credit for U.S. officers.

- **Admission standards:** Military officers are admitted through their service's selection assignment process. International officers and civilians are admitted through an invitational nomination/approval process. To enroll, officers are required to (1) possess a qualifying undergraduate degree or meet academic credentials requirements through a foreign credential evaluation and (2) provide an acceptable score on the TOEFL, if they are not from an English-speaking country. They are also required to have completed appropriate prior PME and possess a Secret security clearance.

Graduation standards: Students complete 39 to 41 credits, including a thesis, with a minimum grade of B– in all courses. Failure to graduate is rare.

Faculty appointment practices: Roughly half of the faculty are active-duty military and usually serve for two years. Civilian faculty operate by reappointment in the Administratively Determined system and are not offered tenure.

External funding: None reported.

MARINE CORPS WAR COLLEGE

Educational focus: The Marine Corps War College (MCWAR) is the senior-level PME institution for the Marine Corps. MCWAR educates senior military officers and civilians to be critical and creative thinkers, military strategists, joint warfighters, and strategic leaders.

Degree programs: Master of Strategic Studies. Ten-month in-residence education. JPME-II credit for U.S. officers.

Non-degree programs and other activities: None.

- **Admission standards:** Military officers are admitted through their service's selection assignment process. International officers and civilians are admitted through an invitational nomination/approval process. To enroll, officers are required to (1) possess a qualifying undergraduate degree or meet academic credentials requirements through a foreign credential evaluation and (2) provide an acceptable score on the TOEFL, if they are not from an English-speaking country. They are also required to have completed appropriate prior PME and possess a Top Secret security clearance.
- **Graduation standards:** Students complete 33 semester credits including an independent research project and pass oral exams. Students must achieve a grade of B− or higher on each academic course. Failure to graduate is rare.

Faculty appointment practices: Military faculty typically rotate in and out every three or four years. Civilian faculty operate by reappointment in the Administratively Determined system and are not offered tenure.

External funding: None reported.

See Tables A.12–A.14.

TABLE A.12

MCU Enrolled Students

ACADEMIC YEAR (AY)	CSC				MCWAR			
	2019	2020	2021	2022	2019	2020	2021	2022
U.S. Army	23	22	22	21	4	4	5	4
U.S. Navy	11	12	16	10	0	1	2	2
U.S. Marine Corps	109[a]	109	106	110	13	12	12	13
U.S. Air Force	21	19	21	19	4	4	4	4
U.S. Space Force	0	0	0	1	0	0	0	0
U.S. Coast Guard	2	1	1	1	1	1	1	1
Foreign military	31	30	30	32	3	3	4	3
DoD civilian	7	7	6	8	1	1	1	3
Other civilian	8	12	11	7	3	4	3	2
Total	212	212	213	209	29	30	32	32

SOURCE: MCU response to request for information.
[a] This group included six enlisted students. Enrollment of enlisted personnel was subsequently discontinued.

TABLE A.13

MCU Personnel

	MCWAR FACULTY		CSC FACULTY		OTHER FACULTY (SAW AND EWS)		MCU STAFF	
	FULL TIME	PART TIME	FULL TIME	PART TIME	FULL TIME	PART TIME	FULL TIME	PART TIME
DoD military officers	4	0	20	0	36	0	41	0
DoD civilians	4	0	23	0	9	0	75	0
Other USG civilians	1	0	0	0	0	0	0	0
Other civilians	0	0	1	0	0	0	39	0
Enlisted	0	0	0	0	0	0	0	0
International military officers	0	0	1	0	0	0	0	0
Total	9	0	45	0	45	0	155	0

SOURCE: MCU response to request for information.

TABLE A.14

MCU Expenditures, FY 2019—2021 ($ millions)

	FY 2019	FY 2020	FY 2021	FY 2022
CSC				
Military personnel[a]	$3.1	$3.5	$3.6	$4.1
Civilian personnel	$3.8	$3.9	$4.0	$4.0
Operations and maintenance	$0.4	$0.3	$0.2	$0.2
Total	$7.3	$7.7	$7.8	$8.3
MCWAR				
Military personnel[a]	$0.5	$0.7	$0.8	$0.8
Civilian personnel	$0.9	$0.9	$0.9	$0.9
Operations and maintenance	$0.7	$0.6	$0.2	$0.3
Total	$2.1	$2.2	$1.9	$2.0

SOURCE: MCU response to request for information.
[a] The authors estimated military personnel costs for Marine Corps personnel based on personnel count and rank, using the "DoD Composite Standard Pay Rate" for Marine Corps personnel from each fiscal year's "Department of Defense (DoD) Military Personnel Composite Standard Pay and Reimbursement Rates," available at Under Secretary of Defense (Comptroller), "Financial Management," webpage, undated.

National Defense University[13]

National Defense University (NDU) in Washington, D.C., is home to five colleges and four research centers (Figure A.5). Each is described in the following section, along with further information about graduation and admission standards, academic programs, faculty, student enrollment, and budget.

Educational focus: The mission of NDU is to "educate Joint Warfighters and other national security leaders in critical thinking and the creative application of military power to inform national strategy and globally integrated operations, under conditions of disruptive change, in order to prevail in war, peace, and competition."[14]

Major organizational units:

NDU maintains five schools with the common purpose to "Provide for the Common Defense":

- The **National War College** educates joint, interagency, and international leaders and warfighters by conducting a senior-level course of study in national security strategy, preparing graduates to function at the highest levels of strategic leadership in a complex, competitive, and rapidly evolving strategic environment.
- The **Eisenhower School** (formerly the Industrial College of the Armed Forces) educates joint warfighters and other national security leaders for strategic leadership and success in developing national security strategy and in evaluating, marshaling, and managing resources to execute that strategy.
- The **Joint Forces Staff College (JFSC)** is composed of three schools:

FIGURE A.5

National Defense University, Main Entrance, Washington, D.C.

---

[13] Information in this section is derived from NDU's responses to the project's requests for information and National Defense University, homepage, undated.

[14] National Defense University, "Vision & Mission," webpage, undated.

- **JAWS** produces joint operational artists fully prepared to serve as senior planners, joint leaders, and advisors at OSD, the Joint Staff, or a four-star CCMD/Sub-Unified Command.
- The **Joint and Combined Warfighting School (JCWS)** educates national security professionals to plan and execute joint, interagency, intergovernmental, and multinational operations. Graduates have a primary commitment to joint, interagency, intergovernmental, and multinational teamwork, attitudes, and perspectives.
- The **Joint Command, Control, and Information Operations School** educates and prepares military officers, senior non-commissioned officers, and their civilian equivalents to enter the Joint Information Operations Command, Control, Communications, Computers, and Intelligence and cyber workforce at the tactical and operational level.

- The **College of Information and Cyberspace (CIC)** educates national security leaders and the cyber workforce on the cyber domain and information environment to lead, advise, and advance national and global security.
- The **College of International Security Affairs (CISA)** educates joint warfighters and national security leaders in creative and critical thinking for the strategic challenges of winning strategies for the contemporary security environment.

NDU maintains four research centers:

- The **Center for Strategic Research** conducts research on regional and functional topics based on DoD strategic guidance as indicated in the National Security Strategy, National Defense Strategy, National Military Strategy, and the National Defense University Strategic Plan.
- The **Center for the Study of Chinese Military Affairs** serves as a national focal point and resource center for research and analytic exchanges on the national goals and strategic posture of the People's Republic of China and its ability to develop, field, and deploy an effective military instrument.
- The **Center for the Study of Weapons of Mass Destruction** is charged with preparing the joint warfighter and select others to address the challenges posed by weapons of mass destruction.
- **NDU Press** publishes INSS research monographs and policy briefs. The press also publishes two professional journals, *Joint Force Quarterly* for the CJCS and *PRISM*, as well as other educational material by and for college faculty and students.

NDU administration includes four primary support units:

- **The Office of the University President.** The NDU president has overall responsibility for NDU's education, research, engagement, and operations. Additional staff within this office include the Senior Vice President, General Counsel, the Director of Strategic Communications, the Capstone Director and staff, Executive Officer and Front Office staff, and the Vice President for Accreditation and Strategic Planning.

- **The Vice President for Academic Affairs/Provost** oversees the NDU Library, Institutional Research and the University Registrar, the Center for Applied Strategic Learning, and institutional health and fitness.
- **The Vice President for Operations/Chief Operating Officer** oversees the non-academic functions of the university. This includes the Human Resources Directorate, the Resource Management Directorate, the Facilities and Engineering Directorate, the Information and Technology Directorate, the Security Directorate, and the Operations Directorate.
- **The Board of Visitors.** A Federal Advisory Committee Act constituted advisory Board of Visitors that supports the NDU president in maintaining the academic integrity of the institution. (This unit is being reconstituted as of January 2022 after DoD discontinued all advisory committees in February 2021.)

Degree programs: NDU offers nine JPME-II and degree programs:

- *JPME-II and Master's Degree in National Security Strategy,* delivered via the National War College over 10.5 months and in-residence
- *JPME-II and Master of Science Degree in National Resource Strategy,* delivered via the Eisenhower School over 10.5 months and in-residence
- *JPME-II and Master of Science Degree in Joint Campaign Planning and Strategy,* delivered via JAWS over 10.5 months and in-residence
- *JPME-II* (no master's degree), delivered via JCWS over ten weeks and four sessions annually, and both in-residence and satellite
- *JMPE-II* (no master's degree), delivered via the JCWS-Hybrid over 40 weeks annually (37 weeks online and three weeks in-residence)
- *JPME-II and Master's Degree in Strategic Information and Cyberspace Studies,* delivered via CIC over 10.5 months and in-residence
- *JPME-II and Master's Degree in Strategic Security Studies,* delivered via CISA over 10.5 months and in-residence
- *Master's Degree in Strategic Information and Cyberspace Studies* (no JPME-II), delivered via CIC over up to five years, and both in-resident and online
- *Joint Special Operations Master of Arts* (no JPME-II), delivered via CISA over ten months and in-residence.

Non-degree programs and other activities: NDU offers multiple non-degree courses and certificates.

There are three General Officer & Flag and Senior Enlisted Leader Courses:

- The *Capstone* course provides required executive education (JPME-III) for newly appointed flag officers and senior civilian national security leaders.
- The *Keystone* course prepares Command Senior Enlisted Leaders for assignment to a General/Flag Officer Joint Headquarters and complements the Capstone course.

- The *Pinnacle* course builds on the knowledge imparted by the Capstone course and runs two times per year.
- *CIC* offers five certificates:
  - Chief Financial Officer Certificate
  - Chief Information Officer Certificate
  - Chief Information Security Officer Certificate
  - Cyber-Leadership Certificate
  - IT Program Management Certificate.
- *CISA* offers three programs and courses:
  - Homeland Defense Fellowship Program
  - Nuclear Energy and Security Program
  - Reserve Component National Security Course.
- The *Center for the Study of Weapons of Mass Destruction* offers one program:
  - Program for Emerging Leaders.
- JFSC offers four non-degree courses:
  - Joint Command, Control, Communications, Computers and Intelligence/Cyber Staff and Operations Course
  - Joint Information Operations Orientation Course
  - Joint Information Operations Planner's Course
  - Joint Military Deception Training Course.
- The International Student Management Office manages the *International Fellows* Programs, delivering services through three primary avenues:
  - The Student Services and Support Program, which provides all supporting services to International Fellows that a service or agency would provide for a U.S. student
  - The Field Studies and Academic Program, which delivers an intensive experiential learning program for International Fellows
  - The Alumni, Outreach, and Engagement Program, which book-ends an International Fellow's time in the program.

Admissions standards: The school itself does not play a role in determining which students attend—the services and agencies provide the names of those who will attend. Students must have earned a bachelor's degree or equivalent for all of the degree programs, but otherwise, there are no other minimum requirements.

Graduation standards: Across the five schools, graduation standards are uniform. Among JPME-II programs, a B or higher grade is required in all core courses, in addition to the successful completion of either a capstone research paper/publishable essay or oral examination(s). NDU disenrolls a few students each year, largely at their request, but this number is very small.

Faculty appointment practices: Military faculty typically rotate in and out. Civilian faculty, under Title 10, can be appointed for up to five years, but in practice they are often appointed for three years at a time. Some adjunct faculty are utilized, but primary faculty utilization is through appointment system. An emphasis for all faculty is placed on both teaching and conducting research.

External funding: NDU has received two DoD Minerva research grants, awarded in 2019 for use in the 2020–2022 period. The first was for $323,731; the second was for $151,834.

See Tables A.15–A.20.

TABLE A.15

NDU Students Enrolled, 2019—2022 (part 1)

CATEGORY	CIC, JPME-II AND MASTER'S				CIC, MASTER'S				CIC, CERTIFICATES				CISA, JPME-II AND MASTER'S			
	2019	2020	2021	2022	2019	2020	2021	2022	2019	2020	2021	2022	2019	2020	2021	2022
U.S. Army	3	7	8	8	37	26	20	10	40	22	22	24	4	5	5	4
U.S. Navy	2	4	4	3	28	16	10	3	44	18	12	8	2	3	2	2
U.S. Marine Corps	1	2	3	3	10	7	6	4	7	2	4	2	1	1	1	1
U.S. Air Force	3	3	4	4	25	14	8	3	35	9	7	4	6	6	6	6
U.S. Coast Guard	1	1	1	1	3	2	2	0	0	0	2	3	1	1	1	1
U.S. Space Force	0	0	0	0	0	0	0	0	0	0	0	0	0	0	0	0
International military	1	8	12	17	3	2	1	0	11	3	1	3	38	37	33	44
DoD civilian	4	3	2	5	185	132	103	61	143	71	57	78	3	4	1	3
Other civilian	2	2	7	8	65	50	7	19	40	27	14	36	9	9	6	9
Total	17	30	41	49	356	249	157	100	320	152	119	158	64	66	55	70

SOURCE: NDU response to request for information.
NOTE: In this table, "Other civilian" includes non-DoD U.S. government personnel and industry personnel. In AY 2022, there were six industry personnel enrolled; in AY 2021, there were seven industry personnel enrolled; in AY 2020, there were ten industry personnel enrolled; and in AY 2019, there were 23 industry personnel enrolled. In this table, "International military" also includes international civilians. In AY 2022, there were four international civilians enrolled; in AY 2021, there were five international civilians enrolled; in AY 2020, there were eight international civilians enrolled; in AY 2019, there were eight international civilians enrolled.

TABLE A.16

NDU Students Enrolled, 2019—2022 (part 2)

CATEGORY	CISA, MASTER'S				CISA, CERTIFICATES				NATIONAL WAR COLLEGE, JPME-II AND MASTER'S				EISENHOWER SCHOOL, JPME-II AND MASTER'S			
	2019	2020	2021	2022	2019	2020	2021	2022	2019	2020	2021	2022	2019	2020	2021	2022
U.S. Army	42	42	27	30	122	81	74	110	42	43	41	40	60	61	59	59
U.S. Navy	1	0	0	0	54	42	38	51	13	14	20	21	24	23	29	29
U.S. Marine Corps	5	5	4	0	0	0	1	1	16	16	16	16	17	15	15	14
U.S. Air Force	9	16	13	0	142	85	87	159	45	43	41	38	56	57	56	51
U.S. Coast Guard	0	0	0	0	38	31	26	36	2	2	2	2	4	4	4	4
U.S. Space Force	0	0	0	0	0	0	0	0	0	0	0	3	0	0	0	4
International military	4	4	2	2	15	12	1	16	32	33	32	35	40	37	35	41
DoD civilian	0	1	1	0	3	2	0	2	19	20	20	19	55	54	49	56
Other civilian	5	5	8	4	3	2	1	2	35	35	38	35	42	40	36	46
Total	66	73	55	36	377	255	228	377	204	206	210	209	298	291	283	304

SOURCE: NDU response to request for information.

TABLE A.17

NDU Students Enrolled, 2019—2022 (part 3)

CATEGORY	JAWS, JFSC, JPME-II AND MASTER'S				JCWS, JFSC, JPME-II, RESIDENT AND SATELLITE DELIVERY				JCWS, JFSC, JPME-II, HYBRID DELIVERY				FLAG AND SENIOR NONCOMMISSIONED OFFICER COURSES			
	2019	2020	2021	2022	2019	2020	2021	2022	2019	2020	2021	2022	2019	2020	2021	2022
U.S. Army	11	11	10	11	253	187	221	178	94	100	100	90	100	54	41	65
U.S. Navy	6	6	7	5	170	159	181	123	39	37	35	42	64	39	29	60
U.S. Marine Corps	2	2	3	3	46	45	45	36	18	22	22	26	23	15	10	26
U.S. Air Force	13	12	10	10	244	233	229	187	76	75	81	78	84	57	46	60
U.S. Coast Guard	1	1	1	1	3	8	10	10	2	10	4	8	12	7	7	12
U.S. Space Force	0	0	0	1	0	0	5	8	0	0	0	0	0	0	0	5
International military	1	2	8	9	54	50	20	26	0	0	0	0	28	16	0	10
DoD civilian	4	4	2	2	18	13	16	11	6	5	3	2	15	3	1	0
Other civilian	0	5	4	2	0	0	1	1	0	1	0	0	9	16	1	2
Total	38	43	45	44	788	695	728	580	235	250	245	246	335	207	135	240

SOURCE: NDU response to request for information.

TABLE A.18

NDU Students Enrolled, 2019—2022 (part 4)

CATEGORY	CENTER FOR STUDY OF WEAPONS OF MASS DESTRUCTION— PROGRAM FOR EMERGING LEADERS				JOINT COMMAND AND CONTROL AND INFORMATION OPERATIONS SCHOOL COURSES, JFSC			
	2019	2020	2021	2022	2019	2020	2021	2022
U.S. Army	14	13	11	11	141	118	69	83
U.S. Navy	7	9	9	8	93	64	37	46
U.S. Marine Corps	1	1	1	1	32	30	34	23
U.S. Air Force	15	17	17	17	31	36	21	18
U.S. Coast Guard	1	2	2	1	1	4	0	1
U.S. Space Force	0	0	0	0	0	0	0	0
International military	0	0	1	1	4	6	1	1
DoD civilian	9	9	10	15	47	46	51	21
Other civilian	27	26	27	22	5	3	1	2
Total	74	77	79	76	354	307	214	195

SOURCE: NDU response to request for information.

TABLE A.19

NDU Personnel (as of November 2021)

STAFF CATEGORY	FACULTY		STAFF	
	FULL TIME	PART TIME (FTE)	FULL TIME	PART TIME (FTE)
DoD military officers	117	0	42	0.3
DoD military enlisted	0	0	17	0
DoD civilians	100	0.5	267	0.8
Other civilians	35	1.1	4	0
International military officers	1	0	0	0
Total	253	1.6	330	1.1

SOURCE: NDU response to request for information.
NOTE: Faculty and staff numbers are rounded to one decimal place.

TABLE A.20

NDU Expenditures, FY 2019–2022 ($ millions)

PROGRAM	FY 2019	FY 2020	FY 2021	FY 2022
Military personnel		Provided by services		
Civilian personnel	48.9	47.4	49.5	45.8
Operations and maintenance	44.1	53.3	46.8	46.9
Total	93.0	100.7	96.3	92.6

SOURCE: NDU response to request for information.

Naval War College[15]

The Naval War College (NWC) operates the Naval PME enterprise at Naval Station Newport, Rhode Island (Figure A.6). NWC utilizes a single faculty for its intermediate- and senior-level PME programs. It enrolls three separate cohorts each academic year. NWC's officer education and research components include the following:

- **College of Naval Command and Staff** (CNC&S)
- **College of Distance Education** (CDE)
- **College of Naval Warfare** (CNW)
- **College of Maritime and Operational Warfare** offers officers and enlisted a variety of non-degree educational opportunities on the maritime operational level. It provides assistance, in residence and on site, to improve the ability of Fleet Commanders and their staffs to plan, prepare, and employ naval, joint, and combined forces across the range of military operations.
- **International Programs** offer PME for foreign students.

---

[15] Information in this section is derived from NWC's responses to the project's requests for information and U.S. Naval War College, homepage, undated.

FIGURE A.6

Naval War College, Main Entrance, Newport, Rhode Island

- **College of Leadership and Ethics** offers intermediate and senior military officers a series of courses on matters such as self-awareness, complex decisionmaking, peer relationships, and institutional accountability.
- **Center for Naval Warfare Studies** conducts research on matters pertaining to war, statesmanship connected with war, and the prevention of war. It includes the War Gaming Department, the Strategic and Operational Research Department, the Stockton Center for International Law, and the Institute for Future Warfare Studies.

NWC also includes other components that address enlisted education and various support units.

External funding: In FY 2021, a faculty member received a $60,000 grant. In FY 2020, CNC&S received a $65,000 grant. In the last two years, NWC received $3.1 million from the Naval War College Foundation.

Below, we provide details for CNC&S, CDE, and CNW.

COLLEGE OF NAVAL COMMAND AND STAFF AND COLLEGE OF DISTANCE EDUCATION

Educational focus: CNC&S is the intermediate-level PME institution for the Navy. CNC&S teaches campaigns and war strategies, theater-level leadership and decisionmaking, and operational planning. CDE offers three distance learning modalities for the CNC&S program.

Research centers: CNC&S incorporates research into its educational activities and does not have dedicated research centers.

Degree programs: The ten-month in-residence program leads to the Master of Defense and Strategic Studies. Non-resident students participating in CDE's fleet seminar program have the option to obtain the master's degree. JPME-I credit for U.S. officers is granted for both the in-residence and distance learning programs.

Non-degree programs and other activities:

- **CDE** offers non-degree JPME-I credit in three modalities: evening seminars at 19 locations (Fleet Seminar Program); courses for students enrolled at NPS in Monterey, California; and an online program.
- **Advanced Strategist Program** offers students in the CNC&S's master's degree program additional credit enabling specialization in the practice of formulating, developing, and executing strategy at various leadership levels. Students enroll in a 13-month advanced program.
- **Maritime Advanced Warfighting School** (MAWS) offers students in the CNC&S's master's degree program additional credit in order to develop strategic and operational leaders with the skills required to plan, execute, and assess combined, joint, and naval operations. Students enroll in a 13-month advanced program.
- Additional certificates are offered in
  - **Ethics and Emergency Military Technology**
  - **Maritime History**
  - **Humanitarian Assistance and Disaster Relief**
  - **Leadership and Ethics.**

Admission standards: Students are selected to attend in residence by their service selection process. The Navy's selection process is not centralized but instead is career-field specific. Officers applying to a CDE program are selected based on their academic accomplishments and potential to complete the program. Fleet seminar program participants desiring to obtain a master's degree must apply and submit reference letters. To enroll in a degree program, officers are required to possess an undergraduate degree.

Graduation standards: Students must achieve a grade of B– or higher on each core academic course and complete the required number of elective courses to earn the master's degree. Failure to graduate is rare.

Faculty appointment practices: Faculty are a mix of active military, retired military practitioners, and civilian academics. All civilian faculty are in the Administratively Determined system. All teaching faculty are part of a tenure system at NWC.

COLLEGE OF NAVAL WARFARE

Educational focus: The College of Naval Warfare (CNW) is the senior-level PME institution for the Navy. CNW educates senior military officers and civilians on national security and strategic studies, including war and grand strategy, strategic-level leadership and decisionmaking, and theater-strategic military planning.

Degree programs: Master of National Security and Strategic Studies. Ten-month in-residence education. JPME-II credit is available for U.S. officers.

Non-degree programs and other activities:

- **Advanced Strategist Program** offers students in the CNW's master's degree program additional credit (similar to the program for CNC&S students). Students enroll in a 13-month advanced program.
- Similar to CNC&S, additional certificates are offered in
  - **Ethics and Emergency Military Technology**
  - **Maritime History**
  - **Humanitarian Assistance and Disaster Relief**
  - **Leadership and Ethics.**

Admission standards: Students are selected to attend in residence by their service selection process. The Navy's selection process is not centralized but instead is career-field specific. To enroll in a degree program, officers are required to possess an undergraduate degree.

Graduation standards: Students must achieve a grade of B– or higher on each core academic course and complete the required number of elective courses to earn the master's degree. Failure to graduate is rare.

Faculty appointment practices: Faculty are a mix of active military, civilian practitioners, and civilian academics. All civilian faculty are in the Administratively Determined system. All teaching faculty are part of a tenure system at CNW.

See Tables A.21–A.23.

TABLE A.21

NWC Enrolled Students

	CNC&S NON-RESIDENT (CDE) NON-DEGREE SEEKING				CNC&S NON-RESIDENT (CDE) DEGREE SEEKING				CNC&S IN-RESIDENCE DEGREE SEEKING				CNW IN-RESIDENCE DEGREE SEEKING			
	2019	2020	2021	2022	2019	2020	2021	2022	2019	2020	2021	2022	2019	2020	2021	2022
U.S. Army	93	98	110	85	4	1	2	10	62	69	74	64	51	48	55	46
U.S. Navy	1,171	1,235	732	1,116	87	102	87	441	112	106	106	99	44	44	38	37
U.S. Marine Corps	77	83	61	66	4	8	3	25	21	20	22	21	18	19	19	15
U.S. Air Force	7	8	10	15	0	3	0	1	28	29	27	25	28	26	27	23
U.S. Space Force	0	0	0	0	0	0	0	0	0	0	1	3	0	0	0	3
U.S. Coast Guard	132	135	88	96	15	17	24	76	4	4	5	4	3	3	3	3
Foreign military	0	0	0	0	0	0	0	0	67	53	59	55	54	37	49	47
DoD civilian	89	92	102	0	0	0	0	106	7	8	7	8	13	15	14	14
Other civilian	221	219	207	0	3	1	2	213	7	9	7	6	11	12	12	11
Total students enrolled	1,790	1,870	1,310	1,378	113	132	118	872	308	298	308	285	222	204	217	199

SOURCE: NWC response to request for information.

TABLE A.22

NWC Personnel

	CNW/CNC&S		CDE		OTHER FACULTY		STAFF (NON-FACULTY)	
	FULL TIME	PART TIME	FULL TIME	PART TIME	FULL TIME	PART TIME	FULL TIME	PART TIME
DoD military officers	52	0	0	0	52	0	19	0
DoD civilians	95	0	57	331[a]	136	0	185	0
Other U.S. government civilians	0	0	0	0	0	0	0	0
Other civilians	0	0	0	0	0	0	0	0
Enlisted	0	0	0	0	0	0	70	0
International military officers	2	0	0	0	0	0	0	0
Total	149	0	57	331[a]	188	0	274	0

SOURCE: NWC response to request for information.
[a] CDE part-time personnel reflects number of adjunct positions, not FTE equivalent.

TABLE A.23

NWC Expenditures, FY 2019—2021 ($ millions)

	FY 2019	FY 2020	FY 2021	FY 2022
CNC&S				
Military personnel	$3.6	$4.2	$4.8	$4.9
Civilian personnel	$10.3	$9.6	$10.5	$11.6
Operations and maintenance	$1.1	$1.1	$1.2	$1.3
Total	$15.0	$14.9	$16.5	$17.8
CNW				
Military personnel	$2.4	$2.8	$3.0	$3.2
Civilian personnel	$6.9	$6.0	$6.6	$7.6
Operations and maintenance	$0.8	$0.7	$0.7	$0.8
Total	$10.1	$9.4	$10.4	$11.6

SOURCE: NWC response to request for information.

Technical Institutions

Air Force Institute of Technology[16]

Educational focus: The Air Force Institute of Technology (AFIT), located at Wright-Patterson Air Force Base, Ohio, provides STEM-related masters and doctorate degrees, initial skills training, and technical professional continuing education (Figure A.7). It conducts research related to its technical programs. It is also charged with managing graduate civilian education within the Air Force, including in nontechnical fields, such as medicine and law.

Research centers: AFIT's research program includes centers that are embedded within the academic departments and two stand-alone externally funded centers. Research centers embedded within the academic departments include

- Autonomy and Navigation Center
- Center for Cyberspace Research
- Center for Directed Energy
- Center for Operational Analysis
- Center for Space Research and Assurance
- Center for Technical Intelligence Studies and Research
- Nuclear Expertise for Advancing Technologies Center.

Stand-alone, separately funded research centers include

- **Air Force Cyberspace Technical Center of Excellence**
- **OSD Scientific Test and Analysis Techniques Center of Excellence** (providing assistance to major acquisition programs in the application of scientific test and analysis techniques).

FIGURE A.7

Air Force Institute of Technology, Main Entrance, Wright-Patterson Air Force Base, Ohio

---

[16] Information in this section is derived from AFIT's responses to the project's requests for information and Air Force Institute of Technology, homepage, undated.

Degree programs: AFIT offers 24 STEM master's degree programs, including aeronautical engineering, nuclear engineering, cyber systems, space systems, logistics, and many others. Some of AFIT's master's degree programs are offered through distance learning. AFIT also offers 14 Ph.D. in-residence programs in related fields.

Non-degree programs and other activities:

- **Graduate School of Engineering and Management** provides 15 graduate certificate programs in addition to its degree programs.
- **The Civil Engineer School** provides technical and management-oriented initial skills training and professional continuing education in civil engineering fields.
- **The School of Systems and Logistics** provides initial skills training and professional continuing education in data analytics, acquisition management, contracting, financial management, logistics management, and systems and software engineering.
- **The School of Strategic Force Studies** provides professional continuing education in nuclear deterrence policy and theory, nuclear command, control, and communications, and cyberspace operations.

Admission standards: Admission to the master's degree programs requires a minimum undergraduate GPA of 3.0 and a minimum GRE score of 153 verbal and 148 quantitative. Each program also has program-specific mathematics coursework requirements. Admission to the Ph.D. programs requires a minimum undergraduate GPA of 3.0, a master's degree in a relevant field with a minimum GPA of 3.5, and a minimum GRE score of 156 verbal and 151 quantitative. Certain international students must also provide an acceptable score on the TOEFL.

Graduation standards: Master's degree students must complete 36 hours of credits (on the quarter system) with a minimum cumulative GPA of 3.00, successfully complete a thesis or independent investigation on a topic approved by the department, and receive a recommendation from the faculty council. Ph.D. students must complete 36 hours of credits beyond the master's degree with a minimum cumulative GPA of 3.00, complete the examination in their specialty area, complete a mathematics requirement, and successfully complete a dissertation on an approved research project.

Faculty appointment practices: Faculty are a roughly equal combination of civilian and active-duty members. Most active-duty faculty teach for three to four years. Graduate school civilian faculty may receive tenure (permanent civil service) after two initial three-year term appointments. Continuing education school faculty are in the General Schedule personnel system. AFIT does not use adjunct/visiting faculty.

External funding: FY 2020: approximately $8,106,000. FY 2021: approximately $8,300,000. Major sources include the Department of Homeland Security, DoD (including Director, Operational Test and Evaluation and Director of Research and Engineering), the U.S. Space Force Space and Missiles Systems Center, and NASA. External funding includes only sources outside of the Air Force and does not include over

$20 million per year in additional research funding from Air Force organizations outside of AFIT's chain of command.
See Tables A.24–A.27.

TABLE A.24

AFIT Graduate School of Engineering and Management Enrolled Students

	CERTIFICATE ONLY (NON-DEGREE)				MASTER'S DEGREE				PH.D. DEGREE				TOTAL			
	2019	2020	2021	2022	2019	2020	2021	2022	2019	2020	2021	2022	2019	2020	2021	2022
U.S. Army	22	29	39	28	15	15	13	13	5	6	6	4	35	45	52	42
U.S. Navy	1	1	0	0	1	0	0	0	0	0	0	0	2	1	0	0
U.S. Marine Corps	0	0	1	0	6	9	8	8	0	0	0	0	6	9	9	8
U.S. Air Force	80	96	168	225	469	502	490	452	81	88	98	79	629	690	743	732
U.S. Space Force	0	0	0	4	0	0	0	48	0	0	0	11	0	0	0	63
U.S. Coast Guard	0	0	0	0	0	1	1	0	0	0	0	0	0	1	1	0
Foreign military	0	0	0	0	17	13	4	8	1	1	1	1	18	14	5	9
DoD civilian	64	75	151	144	42	56	75	104	32	34	35	27	156	210	271	274
Other civilian	0	2	22	18	17	28	30	27	15	12	10	11	35	42	64	57
Total students enrolled	167	203	381	419	567	624	621	660	134	141	150	133	881	1,012	1,145	1,185

SOURCE: AFIT response to request for information.

TABLE A.25

AFIT Civil Engineer School, School of Strategic Force Studies, and School of Systems and Logistics, Enrolled Students

	CIVIL ENGINEER CERTIFICATE ONLY (NON-DEGREE)				STRATEGIC FORCE STUDIES CERTIFICATE ONLY (NON-DEGREE)				SYSTEMS AND LOGISTICS CERTIFICATE ONLY (NON-DEGREE)			
	2019	2020	2021	2022	2019	2020	2021	2022	2019	2020	2021	2022
U.S. Army	32	16	11	27	1	1	1	12	—	15	22	3
U.S. Navy	12	22	6	8	10	0	3	7	—	0	0	2
U.S. Marine Corps	4	4	1	12	3	0	0	1	—	2	4	0
U.S. Air Force	5,744	4,016	4,570	8,068	1,357	716	986	1,346	—	6,275	8,628	6,696
U.S. Space Force	0	17	70	63	0	0	12	62	—	50	84	167
U.S. Coast Guard	5	9	3	7	0	0	0	0	—	0	0	0
Foreign military	0	0	0	0	17	0	0	61	—	4	2	12
Foreign civilian	0	0	0	0	4	0	0	13	—	0	2	0
DoD civilian	6,007	3,511	4,727	5,006	892	359	693	907	—	10,275	13,062	10,301
Other civilian	2	6	1	0	140	2	63	154	—	60	77	65
Total students enrolled	11,807	7,605	9,394	13,191	2,424	1,078	1,758	2,563	—	16,681	21,881	17,246

SOURCE: AFIT response to request for information.
NOTE: — = no data available.

TABLE A.26

AFIT Personnel

	GRADUATE SCHOOL OF ENGINEERING AND MANAGEMENT*		SCHOOL OF SYSTEMS AND LOGISTICS		SCHOOL OF STRATEGIC FORCE STUDIES		CIVIL ENGINEER SCHOOL		AFIT STAFF (NON-FACULTY)	
	FULL TIME	PART TIME	FULL TIME	PART TIME	FULL TIME	PART TIME	FULL TIME	PART TIME	FULL TIME	PART TIME
DoD military officers	76	1	25	0	8	0	17	0	28	0
DoD civilians	77	0	22	0	7	0	12	0	129	0
Other U.S. government civilians	18	1	14	0	0	0	0	0	36	24
Other civilians	7	15	42	0	10	0	15	0	20	0
Enlisted	0	0	0	0	2	0	1	0	26	0
International military officers	1	0	0	0	0	0	0	0	4	0
Total	179	17	103	0	27	0	45	0	243	24

SOURCE: AFIT response to request for information.

AFIT Expenditures, FY 2019—2021 ($ millions)

AFIT	FY 2019	FY 2020	FY 2021	FY 2022
Military personnel (staff)	22.4	27.7	28.7	29.3
Civilian personnel (Air Education and Training Command)	36.7	39.7	40.4	40.5
Operations and maintenance	32.1	35.9	33.1	31.2
Total	91.2	103.3	102.2	101.0

SOURCE: AFIT response to request for information.

U.S. Army Armament Graduate School[17]

The U.S. Army Armament Graduate School (AGS) in Picatinny Arsenal, New Jersey, houses one program designed to enhance the breadth and depth of the armament-related scientific and engineering knowledge base in the U.S. Army Combat Capabilities Development Command—Armaments Center (DEVCOM-AC) workforce (Figure A.8). The program is described in the following section, along with further information about graduation and admission standards, the academic program, faculty, student enrollment, and budget.

Educational focus: The mission of the AGS is to provide advanced-level education and research to enhance the nation's armament capabilities.

Major organizational units:
AGS maintains one school:

- The **AGS** gathers, organizes, and documents armament-specific knowledge through an internally sponsored and internally delivered graduate-level education. The education process was designed to meet succession needs for armament experts and to enhance the capabilities of the scientists and engineers who develop U.S. armaments and related systems.

AGS maintains six key supporting units: the Chancellor, the Office of the Provost/Vice Chancellor for Academic Affairs, the Vice Chancellor for Operations and Finance, the Office of the Registrar/Learning Management System and Database Administrator, the DEVCOM-AC Technical Library, and the DEVCOM-AC Human Research Protection office.

Degree programs: AGS offers one degree program:

- The *Doctor of Philosophy (Ph.D.) in Armament Engineering*, with a course-based non-terminal master's degree in Armament Engineering earned as an interim milestone toward the Ph.D., is an in-residence program focused on enhancing Armament Engineering through learning and research. Congress conferred conditional degree-granting authority to AGS in December 2019.

Non-degree programs and other activities: AGS does not offer any non-degree programs or utilize other activities.

---

[17] Information in this section is derived from AGS's responses to the project's requests for information.

FIGURE A.8

Picatinny Arsenal, New Jersey, Home of the U.S. Army Armament Graduate School

Admissions standards: Admission to AGS is currently limited to qualified DEVCOM–AC engineers, scientists, and mathematicians. AGS maintains a core set of entry requirements that include

- a bachelor's or graduate degree in engineering, physics, chemistry (or other physical science), or mathematics from an accredited college or university or equivalent international degree program
- a demonstrated proficiency, based on strong course performance reflected in their official transcript and in college-level mathematics required by an undergraduate engineering degree
- a recommendation letter from their supervisor
- a personal statement that includes the applicant's current armament engineering interests and plans for dissertation research.

Graduation standards: A Ph.D. candidate must complete 60 credits of coursework (20 three-credit courses) and complete and defend a scientifically and militarily significant, generalizable, original-research dissertation on an armament engineering topic, based on at least 30 credits of original research effort and approved by a committee of nationally recognized experts in related fields.

- A master's degree will be conferred when a student has completed 30 credits toward the Ph.D. requirements, which includes seven three-credit math-intensive core courses and three three-credit courses from a list of Ph.D.-required courses.
- A student who has completed all core courses will take a written and oral preliminary exam over the core curriculum, developed by the core-course instructors.
- A Ph.D. student who has completed master's requirements and passed preliminary exams becomes a Ph.D. candidate upon approval by the faculty research adviser and the select expert dissertation committee of an approved dissertation research proposal.

Faculty appointment practices: No tenure system is used. All faculty are civilians. Additionally, all faculty are adjunct, which is an express mandate from the school's board. Faculty are expected to stay up to date through work experience and utilize that knowledge in the classroom.

External funding: AGS does not have the authority to accept research grants and/or other external funds. As such, it receives no external funding. Competitive internal research awards are available through the Army's In-House Independent Laboratory research program and locally for faculty and dissertation students through the AGS Research program.

See Tables A.28–A.30.

TABLE A.28

AGS Students Enrolled, 2019—2022

CATEGORY	2019	2020	2021	2022
U.S. Army	0	0	0	0
U.S. Navy	0	0	0	0
U.S. Marine Corps	0	0	0	0
U.S. Air Force	0	0	0	0
U.S. Coast Guard	0	0	0	0
U.S. Space Force	0	0	0	0
International military	0	0	0	0
DoD civilian	28	26	36	37
Other civilian	0	0	0	0
Total	28	26	36	37

SOURCE: AGS response to request for information

TABLE A.29

AGS Personnel (as of September 2022)

| STAFF CATEGORY | FACULTY | | STAFF | |
	FULL TIME	PART TIME (FTE)	FULL TIME	PART TIME (FTE)
DoD military officers	0	0	0	0
DoD military enlisted	0	0	0	0
DoD civilians	0	4.6	3.8	0
Other civilians	0	0	1	2.7
International military officers	0	0	0	0
Program total	0	4.6	4.8	2.7

SOURCE: AGS response to request for information.
NOTE: Staff numbers are rounded to one decimal place.

TABLE A.30

Expenditures, FY 2019—2022 ($ millions)

PROGRAM	FY 2019	FY 2020	FY 2021	FY 2022
Military personnel	0	0	0	0
Civilian personnel	2.0	2.0	2.3	2.0
Operations and maintenance	2.9	3.1	2.8	2.3
Total	4.9	5.1	5.1	4.3

SOURCE: AGS response to request for information.
NOTE: Columns may not add to exact totals because of rounding.

Joint Special Operations University[18]

Joint Special Operations University (JSOU) at MacDill Air Force Base in Tampa, Florida, houses one program designed provide intellectual foundations for the work of USSOCOM and special operations forces (SOF) (Figure A.9). The program is described in the following section, along with further information about graduation and admission standards, the academic program, faculty, student enrollment, and budget.

Educational focus: JSOU prepares SOF professionals to address strategic and operational challenges. The university is organized to facilitate the Commander's Title 10 U.S. Code responsibilities and increase the combat readiness of the force. This is accomplished by conducting specialized joint "SOF peculiar" courses of instruction not typically offered in other PME programs.

FIGURE A.9

Entrance to the Joint Special Operations University, MacDill Air Force Base, Tampa, Florida

---

[18] Information in this section is derived from JSOU's responses to the project's requests for information and Joint Special Operations University, homepage, undated.

Major organizational units: JSOU is established as a Direct Reporting Unit Education activity, a subordinate element of USSOCOM. The JSOU President, a Senior Executive Service position (or equivalent designation), reports to the Commander, USSOCOM. JSOU is organized as a Joint-Combined SOFs Polytechnic University, with two major units:

- **College of Special Operations Low-Intensity Conflict (C-SO/LIC)**, which delivers post-secondary joint "SOF peculiar" curricula. C-SO/LIC is also responsible for (1) Enlisted Academy, which provides career-long JPME for noncommissioned officers and (2) the Department of Academic Affairs, responsible for accreditation, academic standards, student support, and education technology.
- **Center for Adaptive Innovative Statecraft** that functions as the USSOCOM intellectual center for research and analysis.

Degree programs: JSOU does not offer any degree programs.

Non-degree programs and other activities: JSOU offers 70 certificate-issuing courses, which are tailored to be SOF-specific in their focus and content.

Admissions standards: Admission to JSOU is determined by USSOCOM priorities.

Graduation standards: To receive a certificate, a student must successfully complete the assigned courses.

Faculty appointment practices: JSOU's faculty is composed of military members, government civilians (Title 10 and Title 5), part-time adjuncts and full-time contractor instructors, and selected guest speakers.

External funding: JSOU does not receive any external funding.
See Tables A.31–A.33.

TABLE A.31

JSOU Students Enrolled, 2019—2022

| | JSOU, CERTIFICATE/NON-DEGREE SEEKING | | | | | | | | | | | |
| | OFFICERS | | | | ENLISTED | | | | CIVILIANS | | | |
CATEGORY	2019	2020	2021	2022	2019	2020	2021	2022	2019	2020	2021	2022
U.S. Army	1,746	2,480	2,401	2,242	1,923	3,063	2,225	2,295	0	0	0	0
U.S. Navy	615	797	638	467	753	935	665	567	0	0	0	0
U.S. Marine Corps	324	365	497	430	528	692	718	701	0	0	0	0
U.S. Air Force	816	735	781	745	972	1,014	810	1,072	0	0	0	0
U.S. Coast Guard	1	8	7	7	3	6	5	2	0	0	0	0
U.S. Space Force	0	25	10	12	0	3	13	6	0	0	0	0
International	1,547	682	855	1,182	553	378	350	473	105	54	136	82
DoD civilian	0	0	0	0	0	0	0	0	1,010	1,683	1,409	1,056
Other civilian	0	0	0	0	0	0	0	0	63	109	133	129
TOTAL	5,049	5,092	5,189	5,085	4,732	6,091	4,786	5,116	1,178	1,846	1,678	1,267

SOURCE: JSOU response to request for information.
NOTE: "DoD civilian" includes general schedule civilians and DoD contractors. "Other civilian" includes U.S. government interagency partners. Enrollment numbers include both residential and distance learning programs.

TABLE A.32

JSOU Personnel (as of September 2022)

| | FACULTY | | STAFF | |
STAFF CATEGORY	FULL TIME	PART TIME (FTE)	FULL TIME	PART TIME (FTE)
DoD military officers	4	0	4	0
DoD military enlisted	18	0	3	0
DoD civilians	22	0	37	0
Other civilians	23	0	49	8
International military officers	0	0	0	0
Program total	67	0	93	8

SOURCE: JSOU response to request for information.

TABLE A.33

JSOU Expenditures, FY 2019—2022 ($ millions)

PROGRAM	FY 2019	FY 2020	FY 2021	FY 2022
Military personnel		Paid by services		
Civilian personnel	7.8	8.2	8.3	8.5
Operations and maintenance	18.2	19.0	19.0	18.8
Total	26.0	27.2	27.3	27.3

SOURCE: JSOU response to request for information.
NOTE: Columns may not add to exact totals because of rounding.

Naval Postgraduate School[19]

The Naval Postgraduate School (NPS), located at Naval Support Activity, Monterey, California, serves the graduate education and applied research needs of the U.S. Navy (Figure A.10).

Educational focus: NPS offers a broad spectrum of defense-focused graduate education and research to advance the operational effectiveness, technological leadership, and warfighting advantage of the U.S. Navy. It also serves the needs of officers and civilians in all the services, other U.S. government agencies, and allied and partner governments. It is also charged with managing graduate civilian education within the Navy.

NPS's schools include the following:

- **Graduate School of Engineering and Applied Sciences**, with programs in applied math, electrical and computer engineering, mechanical and aerospace, meteorology, oceanography, physics, systems engineering, space systems, energy, and undersea warfare
- **Graduate School of Operational and Information Sciences**, with programs in computer science, defense analysis, information sciences, operations research, and cyber
- **Graduate School of Defense Management**, with programs in acquisition management, financial management, management and organizations, manpower and economics, and operations and logistics
- **Graduate School of International and Defense Studies**, with programs in national security affairs, the international graduate program, and the center for security cooperation and support.

Research centers: NPS does not have traditional research centers. However, NPS has interdisciplinary faculty convening on specific subject areas aligned to naval graduate education and applied research needs.
Support units:

- **Faculty Affairs** provides services and support to faculty, administrators, and leadership on the implementation of NPS policies and procedures for academic employees.

---

[19] Information in this section is derived from NPS's responses to the project's requests for information and Naval Postgraduate School, homepage, undated.

FIGURE A.10

Aerial View of the Naval Postgraduate School, Monterey, California

- **Graduate Education Advancement Center** improves the quality of NPS instructional programs by preparing students for their future roles and by working with other agencies to promote the NPS mission.
- **Dean of Students** serves as the Commanding Officer of the Student Military Element responsible for the health, welfare, conduct, and student affairs related to discipline, academic standing, accountability, travel, and military administrative matters.
- **Dudley Knox Library** contributes to learning, research, and teaching through relevant and evolving collections, tools, services, and spaces designed for NPS patrons.
- **Academic Affairs** is the principal organization, under the Provost, responsible for oversight and coordination of the university's graduate education and academic programs.
- **Research Program** provides research and unique research laboratory facilities that permit students and faculty to support Navy/DoD needs.
- **Information Technology and Communications Services** provides network solutions and IT tools tailored to meet the unclassified and classified mission in all facets of teaching, learning, research, and service.
- **Chief Operating Officer** oversees the business operations/staff directorates, which include the Comptroller Office, Command Data Officer, Acquisition Support, Facilities and Property Management, Human Resources, and Travel Office.
- **The Office of University Communications** produces news and information about the institution on education and research programs and significant achievements.
- **Chief of Staff** oversees the special staff directorates which include Command Administration, Equal Employment Opportu-

nity Office, Security Manager, Safety Office, Inspector General, Office of Counsel, and the Staff Judge Advocate Office.

Degree programs: NPS offers approximately 83 graduate degree programs, leading to 83 master's degrees and 15 Ph.D. degrees, in areas as diverse as oceanography, information systems, engineering acoustics, regional security studies, supply chain management, and professional MBAs. In many of the degree programs, NPS offers in-residence and distance learning options.

Non-degree programs and other activities: NPS offers approximately 88 certificates and approximately 12 non-degree professional development programs, in areas such as aviation systems, underwater acoustics, acquisition logistics, and leadership for public administrators.

Admission standards: Interested prospective students first apply for an assessment by NPS. The assessment evaluates the student's prior degree(s), adjusted GPA, and math proficiency. The assessment is sent to the student's service and used by the service to determine whether to sponsor the student. An applicant is eligible to be considered for admission to a degree or a non-degree program if they possess an accredited baccalaureate degree or have completed equivalent academic preparation, as determined by appropriate campus authorities.

Graduation standards: Each degree program maintains its own graduation requirements, including completion of coursework (typically 24–80 quarter-hours) and completion of a thesis, capstone paper or project, or a dissertation (for doctorate degrees). Each program tracks student learning against educational skill requirements to determine mastery of learning. Students must maintain a minimum Graduate Quality Point Rating of 3.00 in all units and a Curriculum Quality Point Rating of 2.75 in all required units. In-residence on-time completion rate is approximately 93 percent.

Faculty appointment practices: The overwhelming majority of the faculty are civilian. Over half of the civilian faculty are tenure track, with the remaining (instructional or research faculty) on renewable term appointments. The military faculty typically rotate in and out every three to four years. There are also four permanent military professors.

External funding: In FY 2020, NPS accepted $36.4 million in reimbursable research projects and $15.3 million in other types of reimbursable activity, such as faculty funding. In FY 2021, NPS accepted $36.6 million in reimbursable research projects and $17.9 million in other types of reimbursable activity. Here are some examples of major funding sources:

- FY 2021 Air Force Operations and Maintenance and RDT&E: $11.5 million total
- FY 2020 Army Operations and Maintenance and RDT&E: $9.2 million total
- FY 2020 defense agencies: $21.8 million total.

See Tables A.34–A.36.

TABLE A.34

NPS Enrolled Students

	CERTIFICATE/NON-DEGREE SEEKING				MASTER'S DEGREE PROGRAM				PH.D. DEGREE PROGRAM			
	2019	2020	2021	2022	2019	2020	2021	2022	2019	2020	2021	2022
U.S. Army	11	8	12	21	211	199	196	164	3	4	7	6
U.S. Navy	96	111	157	164	913	891	886	831	19	16	15	20
U.S. Marine Corps	28	45	48	35	261	292	278	268	3	5	6	5
U.S. Air Force	15	28	33	32	104	108	108	77	4	2	1	3
U.S. Space Force	0	0	0	0	0	0	2	0	0	0	0	0
U.S. Coast Guard	1	1	1	0	10	9	11	12	0	0	0	0
Foreign military	18	15	11	12	123	123	117	151	3	4	5	6
Foreign civilian	0	0	0	0	0	0	0	0	0	0	0	0
DoD civilian	171	176	210	219	394	445	415	349	44	35	36	41
Other civilian	49	41	41	66	223	212	167	181	4	4	5	5
Total students enrolled	389	425	513	549	2,239	2,279	2,180	2,033	80	70	75	86

SOURCE: NPS response to request for information.

TABLE A.35

NPS Faculty

	NPS FACULTY		NPS STAFF	
	FULL TIME	PART TIME	FULL TIME	PART TIME
DoD military officers	36	0	17	0
DoD civilians	459	74	304	0
Other U.S. government civilians	0	0	0	0
Other civilians	45	0	55	0
Enlisted	10	0	31	0
International military officers	0	0	0	0
Total	550	74	407	0

SOURCE: NPS response to request for information.

TABLE A.36

NPS Expenditures, FY 2019–2021 ($ millions)

	FY 2019	FY 2020	FY 2021	FY 2022
NPS—direct Navy funding				
Military personnel	$16.4	$17.3	$18.4	$18.8
Civilian personnel	$63.6	$70.6	$71.2	$62.6
Operations and maintenance	$37.1	$33.4	$29.4	$36.8
Total	$100.7	$104.0	$100.6	$118.2
NPS—reimbursable funding				
Military personnel	$0	$0	$0	$0
Civilian personnel	$73.8	$78.3	$80.4	$79.7
Operations and maintenance	$35.8	$23.1	$22.6	$27.3
Total	$109.6	$101.4	$102.0	$106.9
Grand total	$210.3	$205.4	$202.6	$225.2

SOURCE: NPS response to request for information.
NOTE: Approximately 45–50 percent of reimbursable execution (labor and non-labor) is charged to Navy funding.

Abbreviations

ACSC	Air Command and Staff College	JLA	Joint Learning Area
AFIT	Air Force Institute of Technology	JPME	Joint Professional Military Education
AGS	U.S. Army Armament Graduate School	JPME-I	Joint Professional Military Education, Phase I
AU	Air University	JPME-II	Joint Professional Military Education, Phase II
AWC	Air War College		
AY	academic year	JSOU	Joint Special Operations University
CDE	College of Distance Education	MAWS	Maritime Advanced Warfighting School
CGSOC	Command and General Staff Officers Course	MCU	Marine Corps University
		MCWAR	Marine Corps War College
CIA	Central Intelligence Agency	NDAA	National Defense Authorization Act
CIC	College of Information and Cyberspace	NDRI	National Defense Research Institute
CISA	College of International Security Affairs	NDU	National Defense University
CJCS	Chairman of the Joint Chiefs of Staff	NPS	Naval Postgraduate School
CNC&S	College of Naval Command and Staff	NSRD	National Security Research Division
CNW	College of Naval Warfare	NWC	Naval War College
CSC	Command and Staff College	OBME	outcomes-based military education
DAF	Department of the Air Force	OPMEP	Officer Professional Military Education Policy
DEVCOM-AC	U.S. Army Combat Capabilities Development Command—Armaments Center	OSD	Office of the Secretary of Defense
		OUSD(P&R)	Under Secretary of Defense for Personnel and Readiness
DIA	Defense Intelligence Agency		
DLA	Desired Leader Attribute	PAJE	Process of Accreditation for Joint Education
DoD	Department of Defense		
DoDI	Department of Defense Instruction	PME	professional military education
EWS	Expeditionary Warfare School	ROTC	Reserve Officers' Training Corps
FTE	full-time equivalent	SAASS	School of Advanced Air and Space Studies
FY	fiscal year		
GAO	Government Accountability Office	SAMS	School of Advanced Military Studies
GPA	grade point average	SAW	School of Advanced Warfighting
HASC	House Armed Services Committee	SOF	special operations forces
JAWS	Joint Advanced Warfighting School	STEM	science, technology, engineering, and math
JCS	Joint Chiefs of Staff	TOEFL	Test of English as a Foreign Language
JCWS	Joint and Combined Warfighting School	USAID	United States Agency for International Development
JFSC	Joint Forces Staff College		
JHU SAIS	Johns Hopkins University School of Advanced International Studies	USAWC	United States Army War College
		USSOCOM	U.S. Special Operations Command

References

2021 National Defense Authorization Act—*See* Public Law 116-283.

Air Force Institute of Technology, homepage, undated. As of June 13, 2023:
https://www.afit.edu/

Air University, homepage, undated. As of June 13, 2023:
https://www.airuniversity.af.edu/

Air University, "Office of Sponsored Programs (OSP)," webpage, undated. As of June 13, 2023:
https://www.airuniversity.af.edu/Office-of-Sponsored-Programs/

Bunker, Robert J., "Armed Robotic Systems Emergence: Weapons Systems Life Cycles Analysis and New Strategic Realities," U.S. Army War College, 2017.

Chairman of the Joint Chiefs of Staff Instruction 1800.01E, *Officer Professional Military Education Policy*, May 29, 2015 (superseded).

Chairman of the Joint Chiefs of Staff Instruction 1800.01F, *Officer Professional Military Education Policy*, May 15, 2020.

Chairman of the Joint Chiefs of Staff Memorandum 1810.01E, *Outcomes-Based Military Education Procedures for Officer Professional Military Education*, April 1, 2022.

Chairman of the Joint Chiefs of Staff Memorandum CM-0166-13, *Desired Leader Attributes for Joint Force 2020*, June 28, 2013.

Command and General Staff College, "Command and General Staff College (CGSC)," webpage, undated. As of June 13, 2023:
https://armyuniversity.edu/cgsc/cgsc

Department of Defense Instruction 1300.19, *DoD Joint Officer Management (JOM) Program*, Office of the Under Secretary of Defense for Personnel and Readiness, April 3, 2018.

Department of Defense Instruction 1322.35, *Military Education: Program Management and Administration*, Vol. 1, April 26, 2022.

DoD—*See* U.S. Department of Defense.

DoDI—*See* Department of Defense Instruction.

Dunford, Joseph F., Jr., "Special Areas of Emphasis for Joint Professional Military Education in Academic Years 2020 and 2021," memorandum for the chiefs of the military services and the President, National Defense University, CM-0108-19, May 6, 2019. As of March 8, 2023:
https://www.jcs.mil/Portals/36/Documents/Doctrine/education/jpme_sae_2020_2021.pdf

Farashahi, Mehdi, and Mahdi Tajeddin, "Effectiveness of Teaching Methods in Business Education: A Comparison Study on the Learning Outcomes of Lectures, Case Studies and Simulations," *International Journal of Management Education*, Vol. 16, No. 1, 2018.

Farrell, Brenda S., *Joint Military Education: Actions Needed to Implement DOD Recommendations for Enhancing Leadership Development*, U.S. Government Accountability Office, GAO-14029, October 2013.

Farrell, Brenda S., *Professional Military Education: Programs Are Accredited, but Additional Information Is Needed to Assess Effectiveness*, U.S. Government Accountability Office, GAO-20-323, February 2020.

Healy, Margaret, and Maeve McCutcheon, "Teaching with Case Studies: An Empirical Investigation of Accounting Lecturers' Experiences," *Accounting Education*, Vol. 19, No. 6, 2010.

Hodgson, Quentin E., Charles A. Goldman, Jim Mignano, and Karishma R. Mehta, *Educating for Evolving Operational Domains: Cyber and Information Education in the Department of Defense and the Role of the College of Information and Cyberspace*, RAND Corporation, RR-A1548-1, 2022. As of February 24, 2023: https://www.rand.org/pubs/research_reports/RRA1548-1.html

Joint Chiefs of Staff, "Officer Professional Military Education Policy (OPMEP)," Chairman of the Joint Chiefs of Staff Instruction 1800:01D, July 15, 2009; Ch. 1, December 15, 2011; Directive Current as of September 5, 2012. As of March 8, 2023: https://usacac.army.mil/sites/default/files/documents/cace/LREC/2011_CJCSI_1800.01D_Ch1_OPMEP.pdf

Joint Chiefs of Staff, *Developing Today's Joint Officers for Tomorrow's Ways of War: The Joint Chiefs of Staff Vision and Guidance for Professional Military Education and Talent Management*, May 1, 2020.

Joint Special Operations University, homepage, undated. As of June 13, 2023: https://jsou.edu/

Marine Corps University, homepage, undated. As of June 13, 2023: https://www.usmcu.edu/

Mattis, Jim, *Summary of the 2018 National Defense Strategy of the United States of America: Sharpening the American Military's Competitive Edge*, U.S. Department of Defense, January 2018.

Mayberry, Paul W., Charles A. Goldman, Kimberly Jackson, Eric Hastings, Hannah Acheson-Field, and Anthony Lawrence, *Making the Grade: Integration of Joint Professional Military Education and Talent Management in Developing Joint Officers*, RAND Corporation, RR-A473-1, 2021. As of February 24, 2023: https://www.rand.org/pubs/research_reports/RRA473-1.html

National Defense Authorization Act for Fiscal Year 1994, Public Law 103-160, November 30, 1993.

National Defense University, homepage, undated. As of June 13, 2023: https://www.ndu.edu/

National Defense University, "Vision & Mission," webpage, undated. As of June 17, 2023: https://www.ndu.edu/about/vision-mission/

Naval Postgraduate School, homepage, undated. As of June 13, 2023: https://nps.edu/

Office of the Under Secretary of Defense (Personnel & Readiness), *Department of Defense Report: A Review of Joint Professional Military Education Programs*, Senate Report 114-255, November 14, 2017.

Public Law 116-283, William M. (Mac) Thornberry National Defense Authorization Act for Fiscal Year 2021, January 1, 2021.

Raju, P. K., and Chetan S. Sankar, "Teaching Real-World Issues Through Case Studies," *Journal of Engineering Education*, Vol. 88, No. 4, 1999.

Secretary of the Air Force Public Affairs, "Space Force to Partner with Johns Hopkins University SAIS for Service-Specific IDE, SDE," *Space Force News*, October 26, 2022.

Stewart, Jenice P., and Thomas W. Dougherty, "Using Case Studies in Teaching Accounting: A Quasi-Experimental Study," *Accounting Education*, Vol. 2, No. 1, 1993.

Strategic Studies Institute, "Our Mission," webpage, undated. As of June 13, 2023:
https://ssi.armywarcollege.edu/about/

Under Secretary of Defense (Comptroller), "Financial Management," webpage, undated. As of May 1, 2023:
https://comptroller.defense.gov/Financial-Management/Reports/

U.S. Army, "CGSC Circular 350-1: U.S. Army Command and General Staff College Catalog," 2016.

U.S. Army War College, homepage, undated. As of June 13, 2023:
https://www.armywarcollege.edu/

U.S. Army War College, "Center for Strategic Leadership," webpage, undated. As of June 17, 2023:
https://csl.armywarcollege.edu/Mission.aspx

U.S. Army Heritage and Education Center," Visit Us," webpage, undated. As of June 13, 2023:
https://ahec.armywarcollege.edu/visit.cfm

U.S. Code, Title 10, Subtitle A, Part II, Chapter 38, § 668, Definitions.

U.S. Code, Title 10, Subtitle B, Part III, Chapter 751, § 7414, Degree Granting Authority for United States Army Command and General Staff College.

U.S. Code, Title 31, Subtitle II, Chapter 13, Subchapter III, § 1341, Limitations on Expending and Obligating Amounts.

U.S. Code, Title 31, Subtitle II, Chapter 13, Subchapter III, §1342, Limitation on Voluntary Services.

U.S. Department of Defense, *HASC RFI on Professional Military Education*, June 15, 2022.

U.S. House of Representatives Committee on Armed Services, *Report of the Panel on Military Education*, 101st Congress, April 21, 1989.

U.S. House of Representatives Committee on Armed Services, *Another Crossroads? Professional Military Education Two Decades After the Goldwater-Nichols Act and the Skelton Panel*, H.A.S.C. No. 111-67, May 20, 2009.

U.S. Naval War College, homepage, undated. As of June 13, 2023:
https://usnwc.edu/

Warthen, Lawanda, "The U.S. Army War College Breaks New Ground in Hybrid Education," Army.mil, 2021.

Image Credits

Pg. III: U.S. Air National Guard photo by Master Sgt Mike R. Smith
Pg. IV: U.S. Marine Corps Photo by Sgt Alex Kouns
Pg. V: U.S. Marine Corps photo by Lance Cpl. Kenny Nunez Bigay
Pg. VII: U.S. Air Force photo by Wesley Farnsworth
Pg. VIII: U.S. Air Force photo by R.J. Oriez
Pg. XI: U.S. Air Force photo by R.J. Oriez
Pg. XII: U.S. Air Force photo by Wesley Farnsworth
Pg. XVIII: Marine Corps photo by Kathy Reesey
Pg. 22: U.S. Navy photo by Cmdr. Gary Ross
Pg. 28: U.S. Air Force photo by Cassandra Cornwell
Pg. 30: U.S. Air Force photo by Darius Hutton
Pg. 36: Official U.S. Marine Corps photo by Lance Cpl. Kenny Nunez Bigay
Pg. 44: Master Sgt William Wiseman
Pg. 46: U.S. Air Force photo by R.J. Oriez
Pg. 50: U.S. Air Force photo by Trey Ward
Pg. 52: U.S. Air Force photo by Trey Ward
Pg. 57: U.S. Air Force photo by Melanie Rodgers Cox
Pg. 60: U.S. Air Force photo by Jaima Fogg
Pg. 61: Airman 1st Class Charles Welty
Pg. 62: U.S. Air Force photo by Katie Scott
Pg. 68: U.S. Army photo by Noah Albro
Pg. 73: USAWC staff
Pg. 78: MCU staff
Pg. 82: NDU staff
Pg. 90: NWC staff
Pg. 94: Wesley Farnsworth
Pg. 99: Defense Acquisition University staff
Pg. 101: JSOU staff
Pg. 105: NSP staff

Milton Keynes UK
Ingram Content Group UK Ltd.
UKHW052037100324
439157UK00007B/19

9 781977 411174